Pe   ts

The Famous, Infamous, and Quirky
of the Keystone State

Manufactured in the United States of America

1 2 3 4 5   01 00 99

Library of Congress Cataloging-in-Publication Data

Reynolds, Patrick M.
    Pennsylvania firsts : the famous, infamous, and quirky of the
Keystone State / Patrick M. Reynolds.
        p. cm.
    Includes bibliographical references.
    ISBN 0-940159-46-5 (alk. paper)
    1. Pennsylvania—History—Miscellanea.   I. Title.
    F149.6.F49 1999   98-49234
    974.8—dc21

Unless otherwise noted, all photographs and illustrations are courtesy of
    Patrick M. Reynolds.
Cover and interior design: Jerilyn Bockorick

This book is available at a special discount on bulk purchases for promotional, business, and educational use.

For information write:
Camino Books, Inc.
P.O. Box 59026
Philadelphia, PA 19102

www.caminobooks.com

To my grandsons,
Avery and Michael

CONTENTS

ACKNOWLEDGMENTS

You might wonder where I found all these conjurers of concepts and contraptions. Since 1976 I have been doing an illustrated feature called "Pennsylvania Profiles," which appears weekly in newspapers and magazines across the commonwealth. I do all the research, writing, and drawing for this feature. Thus, not only must I know who did what, but also what the person and his or her gizmo looked like. I've scoured historical societies, libraries, museums, and private collections for words and pictures.

If I were to thank all the many, many people who've taken the time to answer my questions, to open doors and files for me, to show me photos and artwork I never knew existed, the list would be very long indeed. And so I'll just say thank you to all who have helped me over the years.

But there is one person to whom I am particularly grateful. "Pennsylvania Profiles" still appears regularly in *Pennsylvania Magazine*, and I thank its editor, Matthew Holliday, for recommending me to Camino Books.

Patrick M. Reynolds

INTRODUCTION

If it rolls, rocks, fizzes, flames, or foams, it most likely came from Pennsylvania. If you can ride it, fly it, kick it, wear it, swab it, or walk on it, chances are it was invented in the commonwealth. For the past three centuries, the commonwealth has been the home of inventors, innovators, entrepreneurs, and mechanical wizards who have concocted a plethora of procedures, products, knickknacks, doohickeys, and gizmos that make life interesting, if not easier.

Societies are often measured by the advances they make in the arts and sciences, and Pennsylvanians hold the bragging rights to bringing the United States to the forefront of modern civilization. As a matter of fact, Pennsylvania has so many firsts that it needs a companion title, *Philly Firsts* by Janice L. Booker, to do them justice. *Pennsylvania Firsts* wanders beyond the city limits of Philadelphia and concentrates on firsts—from the autogiro to the Zippo—that originated in such places as Pittsburgh, Pottsville, Punxsutawney, and Pithole.

Even with the companion volume on Philadelphia, you will not be able to read about every invention or innovation that came out of Pennsylvania. For a state as steeped in history and as rich in natural and human resources as this one, it would take many volumes to do that.

No, you won't find them all here. But what you will find is a mix of my favorites—those that I think show the ingenuity, the risk-taking, and the genius of the people of the Keystone State, and those that best contributed to the progress of our nation in so many fields: energy and industry, transportation, food, entertainment, politics, education and religion, architecture and sports.

Early Pennsylvania

THE FIRST INHABITANTS

During the summers of 1973, '74, and '75, Dr. James Adovasio, an anthropology professor at the University of Pittsburgh, aided by 14 students, dug and scraped at a hillside in southwestern Pennsylvania trying to find evidence of ancient civilizations. They sent their findings to the Smithsonian Institution in Washington, D.C., for radiocarbon dating.

The results proved that humans lived some 16,240 years ago at the Meadowcroft Rock Shelter, as the site in Washington County was called. This makes Meadowcroft Rock the earliest documented place of human habitation in the Western Hemisphere. And it gave new meaning to a Pennsylvania tourism slogan from the 1980s: *Pennsylvania— America Starts Here.*

THE TRIBES

The early people of Pennsylvania left no written records of who they were, what they did, and exactly where they lived. It was up to archaeologists to dig up evidence that included fragments of bone, stone, pottery, and wooden tools.

When the Europeans arrived at the beginning of the 17th century, Pennsylvania's Indians had developed to the stage that scientists call the Woodland Epoch. They lived in towns, made good pottery, and dressed in comfortable and attractively decorated leather garments. They showed an artistic ability in the carving of ornaments, the weav-

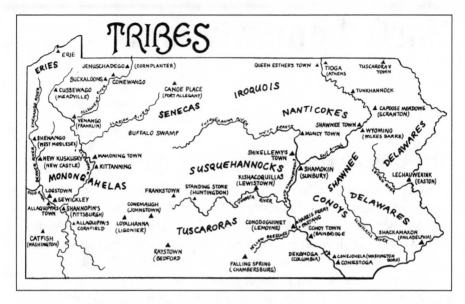

TRIBES

ERIE

ERIES

JENUSCHADEGO (CORNPLANTER)

BUCKALOONS CONEWANGO

CUSSEWAGO
(MEADVILLE)

CANOE PLACE
(PORT ALLEGANY)

VENANGO
(FRANKLIN)

SENECAS

IROQUOIS

QUEEN ESTHERS TOWN

TIOGA
(ATHENS)

TUSCARORA'S
TOWN

TUNKHANNOCK

NANTICOKES

CAPOOSE MEADOWS
(SCRANTON)

SHAWNEE TOWN

WYOMING
(WILKES BARRE)

BUFFALO SWAMP

SHENANGO
(WEST MIDDLESEX)

NEW KUSKUSKY
(NEW CASTLE)

MAHONING TOWN

KITTANNING

SUSQUEHANNOCKS

MUNCY TOWN

SHIKELLEMY'S
TOWN

SHAMOKIN
(SUNBURY)

DELAWARES

LECHAUWEKINK
(EASTON)

MONONGAHELAS

LOGSTOWN

SEWICKLEY

ALLAQUIPPAS SHANNOPIN'S
TOWN (PITTSBURGH)

ALLAQUIPPA'S
CORNFIELD

CONEMAUGH
(JOHNSTOWN)

LOYALHANNA
(LIGONIER)

FRANKSTOWN

STANDING STONE
(HUNTINGDON)

KISHACOQUILLAS
(LEWISTOWN)

TUSCARORAS

JUNIATA RIVER

CONODOGUINET
(LEMOYNE)

CONOYS

DELAWARES

HARRIS FERRY
PAXTANG

CONOY TOWN
(BAINBRIDGE)

SHACKAMAXON
(PHILADELPHIA)

CATFISH
(WASHINGTON)

RAYSTOWN
(BEDFORD

FALLING SPRING
(CHAMBERSBURG)

DEKONOGA
(COLUMBIA)

CONEJOHELA (WASHINGTON
CONESTOGA BORO)

Archaeologists estimate that Native Americans have lived in Pennsylvania for about 18,000 years. Here are some of their villages and tribal areas.

ing of blankets, and the singing and dancing that accompanied their religious rituals.

In the early 1700s there were four major tribes, or nations, of Indians in the commonwealth: the Delawares or Lenni-Lenape, the Susquehannocks, the Eries, and the Monongahelas.

The Delawares

Calling themselves *Lenni-Lenape*, meaning "real men," the Delawares occupied the Delaware basin and were the most important Algonquian-speaking tribe. Their subtribes included the Shawnees, Nanticokes, and Conoys. The Nanticokes were feared because they concocted deadly poisons and practiced witchcraft. Another subtribe, the Munsees, lived in the upper reaches of the Delaware Valley above the Lehigh River, in and around the Pocono Mountains. Treaties with the Quakers and incursions by other whites forced the Delawares to migrate first to the Wyoming Valley near Wilkes-Barre, then to Ontario, Canada, and finally to the western United States. Descendants of the Delawares now live on reservations in Oklahoma and Ontario.

The Susquehannocks

This powerful Iroquoian-speaking tribe, which often fought wars against the Lenni-Lenape, occupied the Susquehanna Valley from central Pennsylvania southward into Maryland. Their subtribes included the Seneca and Tuscarora. The Five Nations of the Iroquois finally annihilated them in 1675. A few stragglers known as the Conestoga Indians were wiped out in a massacre by the Pantang Boys in Lancaster in 1763.

The Eries

The Erie Indians lived south of Lake Erie. Because of the many panthers and wild cats that roamed this region, they were often called the Cat Nation. Not much is known about this tribe except that they were conquered by the Iroquois between 1655 and 1656. A Jesuit missionary at Onondaga (now Syracuse, New York) noted that 600 of the Cat Nation had voluntarily surrendered to the Iroquois.

The Monongahelas

Judging from the graves, post molds, and refuse pits discovered by archaeologists, the most advanced Indians that lived in the upper Ohio Valley, now southwestern Pennsylvania, were the Monongahelas. They disappeared from the face of the earth before anyone came to observe or record them. *Monongahela* is the name given to them by archaeologists because of the abundance of relics attributed to them in the region of the

Monongahela River. The Monongahelas lived in stockaded villages, situated on hilltops. Within the stockades were dome-shaped (beehive) houses arranged in a circle. They lived by farming but their diet was supplemented by hunting and fishing.

THE DISCOVERERS

The first European contacts with the territory that is now Pennsylvania are obscure and indefinite. As early as 1608, Captain John Smith explored the Chesapeake Bay and sailed as far as "the countrey of the Susquehannocks," but most likely did not reach Pennsylvania. In 1609, Henry Hudson, an Englishman working for the Dutch, navigated his ship, the *Half Moon*, into Delaware Bay and claimed the area for the Netherlands. He ran aground before reaching present-day Pennsylvania. When the tide came in, his crew freed the ship and he turned back to the Atlantic.

In 1610, Samuel Argall sailed into the Delaware Bay and claimed it for the governor of Virginia, Lord de la Warr. Captain Cornelius Hendricksen, a Dutchman, ascended the Delaware in 1616, and reached the falls near Trenton, New Jersey, and Bucks County, Pennsylvania. On his way back to the Atlantic, he noticed the mouth of a river that he had missed earlier. He named it *Schuyler Kill*, meaning "hidden river." It is now known as the Schuylkill River.

The First Central Pennsylvania Explorer

From the autumn of 1615 to the spring of 1616, the first exploration of the Susquehanna River for its entire length was made by Etienne (Stephen) Brulé, a Frenchman working for Samuel Champlain, the first governor of New France (which consisted of eastern Canada, all the land west of the Allegheny River, westward beyond the Mississippi to the borders of New Spain—Texas, Utah, California, ending at the Pacific Ocean from Oregon northward to Alaska).

Brulé came to New France with Champlain in 1608. He got along with the Indians, so Champlain persuaded the Algonquian chief to let the young lad live with the tribe and learn its language and customs. Eventually Champlain placed Brulé on salary as his interpreter. Needing allies to fight the Iroquois in upstate New York, Champlain sent Brulé and 12 Hurons to Charntouan, an Indian town near Athens, Greene County, to ask for help. After several days of pow-wows, the Carantouans agreed to help. Brulé and 500 Carantouans trekked north to join Champlain and attack the Iroquois at Onondaga. Meanwhile, Champlain and the Hurons attacked Onondaga without Brulé's reinforcements. Champlain was wounded; his attack was repulsed, and he retreated to Canada.

Brulé and the Carantouans returned to one of their villages at present-day Oneida, New York. From there, in about October 1615, Brulé and a group of Carantouans floated down the north branch of the Susquehanna River and continued south into Maryland to the river's mouth at the Chesapeake Bay. Along the way, he reported meeting many tribes, all of whom welcomed him and hated the Dutch because of their cruelty toward the Indians. Thus, according to Jesuit missionary journals, Brulé was the first white man to explore central Pennsylvania from north to south.

Brulé's return trip up the Susquehanna was even more adventurous. The Iroquois attacked his expedition and everyone scattered. Brulé got lost and wandered into an Iroquois village. The Indians pounced on him, tied him to a stake, and began to torture him. But when they tried to pull a crucifix from around his neck, Brulé threatened them with the wrath of God. Just then a terrific thunderstorm came up. His tormentors ran in all directions. Then the chief released Brulé. After a two-year absence, he finally returned to Champlain in 1618.

THE GRANDFATHER OF PENNSYLVANIA

The man who was the prime mover in the initial colonization of Pennsylvania was not a Dutchman, nor a Swede, nor an English Quaker.

He was a Finn by the name of Klas Fleming. Born in 1592 in Louhisaari, Finland, Fleming moved to Sweden, joined the navy, and rose to the rank of admiral. Fleming entered politics in 1625 as Royal Councillor. When the College of Commerce (Board of Trade) was established in 1637, he became its president. A year later, he landed a directorship in the New Sweden Company, where he used his money and political clout to convince Queen Christina to authorize a colony in the New World.

The First European Settlements in Pennsylvania

The queen hired a Dutchman, Peter Minuit, to explore the east coast of America to find a place to colonize. Minuit was an excellent choice because he had been the governor of New Netherland and was famous for purchasing Manhattan Island from the Indians for $24 worth of cheap jewelry.

Minuit took two ships and two dozen soldiers and sailed to America in the spring of 1638. Again he worked out a deal with the Indians: for a few cases of cloth, tools, and baubles, he bought all their land along the west shore of the Delaware River. He chose a spot at present-day Wilmington, Delaware, and built Fort Christina; he named the place New Sweden. Here Minuit conducted business as the first Swedish governor of Pennsylvania.

On his way back to Sweden, his ship went down in a storm and Minuit drowned. But another ship made it home, and its crew reported the opportunities for trade and wealth awaiting the Swedish people in Pennsylvania.

Queen Christina, needing settlers for her colony, put out a call for people willing to go to America. When nobody volunteered to leave the relative comfort of their homes, towns, and farms to live in a wilderness on the other side of the world, Klas Fleming had an idea. He advised the queen to order her provincial governors to take the prisoners from their jails and send them with their families to New Sweden. They complied. Thus, Pennsylvania's first citizens were convicted criminals!

In 1640, Peter Ridder brought a shipload of settlers to New Sweden. Unfortunately, there were no skilled tradesmen among these ex-cons, and they knew nothing about construction. Unable to build real houses, they lived in holes covered over with sod, or in tepee-like shelters. Yet from these meager dwellings they managed to clear many acres of land and prepare fields for agriculture.

Big Tub

Between the late 1630s and the early 1640s, the Swedish government sent officers to evict the Finns who had illegally crossed the border and were

Statue of Governor Johan Printz at Governor Printz Park in Essington, along the Delaware River.

killing game and chopping down trees. One enforcer who did a superb job in chasing and capturing the Finnish poachers was a retired cavalry officer named Johan Printz. Queen Christina was so impressed by Printz that she knighted him and appointed him governor of New Sweden in 1642.

Governor Printz fitted two ships, the *Fawn* and the *Swan*, with tons of supplies, then set sail for America in the autumn of 1642. Accompanying him were his wife, his daughter, the Reverend John Campanius, and a number of the convicted Finns. His party landed at Fort Christina in February 1643, but Printz did not like the strategic location of the fort. He cruised up the Delaware as far as Trenton. On the way back, he selected Tinicum Island for his settlement. As soon as Printz set foot on land and met the natives, they gave him a nickname, Big Tub, because he stood nearly seven feet tall, weighed over 400 pounds, and had a blustering, dictatorial manner.

THE FIRST SETTLEMENT AND THE FIRST CHURCH

Tinicum Island was the first permanent settlement within the borders of present-day Pennsylvania. Here Governor Printz built a fort of hemlock logs near the water's edge. He called it New Gottenburg and equipped it with four brass cannons. Printz's own residence was a two-story log structure called Printzhof.

The Reverend Campanius built a church on Tinicum Island, which he dedicated on September 4, 1646. This was the first house of worship in Pennsylvania. Campanius also made the first translation of the Lutheran Catechism into the Lenni-Lenape dialect of the Algonquian language. Bowing to the Indian way of life, Campanius altered some of the passages: "Give us this day our daily bread" became "Give us this day a plentiful supply of venison and corn."

☞ *To Visit: Governor Printz Park*

Today the remains of Tinicum and the foundation of Printzhof are preserved in Governor Printz Park in Delaware County, situated just south of Philadelphia International Airport. Administered by the Pennsylvania Historical and Museum Commission, it is dotted with picnic tables and special exhibits. Standing near the water's edge is a bronze statue of Big Tub, Governor Printz.

Governor Printz Park
Hours: Open daily.

THE BEGINNINGS OF PENNSYLVANIA

After the Dutch took control of the area from the Swedes in 1655, Pennsylvania remained a Dutch colony until shortly after King Charles II returned from exile to rule England following the fall of Oliver Cromwell's Protectorate. In 1664, King Charles asserted England's rights to North America, meaning that he intended to take control of the middle colonies—which included all the land from the Canadian border at Vermont, southward to the Maryland boundary at the Potomac River—from the Dutch.

William Penn's father was an admiral in the British navy and saw action in the 1640s and 1650s, when the government was so broke it could not pay its military. Admiral Penn died before he could collect his back pay, amounting to the equivalent of about $16,000. When his son, William, told Charles II in 1681 that he would accept land in America as payment for the debt, the king was delighted. He granted Penn all the land that lay between the 39th and 42nd degrees of north latitude, extending from the Delaware River westward for five degrees of longitude. These boundaries are almost the same as those of the state today.

On March 4, 1681, Charles II signed a charter giving Penn the right to act as proprietor and govern the land in the king's name. In honor of Penn's father, he called the vast tract *Pennsylvania*, meaning "Penn's Woods." Now, except for the king himself, William Penn was the largest landowner in the British empire.

Pennsylvania's First Government

Penn was too busy to sail to America with the first boatload of colonists in 1681, so he appointed his cousin, Captain William Markham, as deputy governor and sent him over to get things organized. Markham's first stop in America was in New York, where he informed officials of Pennsylvania's new status. Then he sailed to Uppland, now Chester, Delaware County, which became the first official capital of Pennsylvania. Markham was authorized to name a council of nine, which convened on August 3, 1681, in Uppland. That date denotes the beginning of civil government in the state.

Philadelphia—Named After an Ancient Turkish City

William Penn wanted to build a great seaport in his colony, and reports indicated that the facilities and shoreline of Uppland were insufficient. Therefore, on September 30, 1681, he appointed four commissioners to find a suitable site and purchase the necessary land on which to build a great city. These commissioners—William Crispin, John Bezar, William Haige, and Nathaniel Allen—promptly set sail for America. Crispin had been named surveyor-general, but he died during the voyage and was replaced by Captain Thomas Holme.

After their arrival here, the commissioners soon discovered that a large number of Swedes held title to most of the land around Uppland. It would take years to buy what they needed for the city, so they started to look farther north. Seven weeks later they found a place between the Delaware and Schuylkill Rivers that was high and dry, and where the Delaware was deep enough for a port. Two Swedes, the Svenson brothers, owned the land and were willing to sell. Governor Penn already had a name in mind for his new city. It would be named after a town in Asia Minor (now Turkey) founded by King Attalus Philadelphus in 159 B.C. In the Lydian language, *Philadelphia* means "Brotherly Love."

Almost a half century before William Penn laid the foundation of the Quaker commonwealth, the Dutch and Swedes had brought Africans to the Delaware Valley as slaves.

William Penn owned slaves. In 1685, Penn instructed his steward at Pennsbury, his estate in what is now Bucks County, to use black slaves because "they could be held for life." Penn was interested in "regulating their morals and marriages and their trials and punishments so they could receive proper treatment while in bondage." However, in 1700, he urged the yearly meeting of the Society of Friends to oppose slavery. Immediately afterwards, the Quakers began to free their slaves. Penn's will stipulated "that my negroes, John and Jane, his wife, shall be set free one month after my decease." He also bequeathed 100 acres of land to another African named Old Sam.

Francis Daniel Pastorius and several other members of the Friends Monthly Meeting in Germantown drafted a strong moral denouncement of slavery and the slave trade in 1688. This was the first protest against slavery in the English colonies. A century later, on March 1, 1780, the Pennsylvania Assembly passed the first state law providing for the emancipation of slaves. The sponsor of that law was an Irish immigrant, George Bryan, who was acting vice president of the state executive council.

☞ To Visit: Pennsbury Manor

During William Penn's first visit to Pennsylvania in 1683, he built a summer home along the banks of the Delaware River north of Philadelphia, near present-day Tullytown. Pennsbury Manor was completely rebuilt in the 1940s and is now a property of the Pennsylvania Historical and Museum Commission.

Pennsbury Manor
400 Pennsbury Memorial Lane
Morrisville, PA 19067
215-946-0400
Hours: Tuesday-Saturday, 9 A.M.-5 P.M.; Sunday, 12-5 P.M.

THE FIRST BOUNDARY SURVEY

The Mason-Dixon Line, which marks the boundary between Pennsylvania and Maryland, was the first precise measurement of land ever made in North America. And it happened because Charles Mason and Jeremiah Dixon were the first to bring to this country two "modern" measuring instruments—a telescope with glass that withstood changes in temperature and moisture, and an astronomical clock that accurately measured vast distances of land by taking into consideration the curvature of the earth.

Establishing the Mason-Dixon Line was necessary because of the short-sightedness of King James I. When the Pilgrims settled in Massachusetts in 1620, they were only the second group of English colonists in America, the

Charles Mason and Jeremiah Dixon conducting their survey of the Pennsylvania and Maryland boundary in 1765. The equipment in the foreground (astronomical clock, sextant, and telescope) was used to find precise locations on the ground by observing the stars. The porters, ax men, and other crew members are in the foreground. *Painting by Patrick M. Reynolds, courtesy of the National Watch and Clock Museum, Columbia, PA*

first being those in Jamestown, Virginia. At the time, King James fixed the northern boundary of the London Company (Jamestown) at latitude 41 degrees north and the southernmost limit of the Plymouth Company (the Pilgrims' territory) at 38 degrees north. This meant that the colonies had a two-degree overlap, which is more than half of what is now Pennsylvania, New Jersey, and most of Maryland! Within this overlap area, the king ruled that neither company was to settle within 100 miles of each other.

Over the next 60 years, subsequent kings of England granted land for colonies within that overlap area, and a squabble ensued between William Penn and Charles Calvert, the Third Lord Baltimore. The king ordered the Royal Board of Trade and Plantations to settle the squabble, and in 1685, it sided with Penn, awarding him all of present-day Delaware. Delaware remained part of Pennsylvania for the next 20 years, until it seceded and formed its own government.

Lord Baltimore's heirs never accepted the Board's decision. They wanted all the land northward to the 40th degree of latitude, and in 1732 and 1750, they filed two more suits against Penn's heirs. Each time, the Board ruled in favor of the Penn family. Hard feelings between the colonies of Pennsylvania and Maryland continued to fester.

Meanwhile, two men were making names for themselves in the scientific community in England. From 1756 to 1760, Charles Mason was an assistant observer at the Greenwich Observatory, where he helped the Astronomer Royal, Charles Bradley, catalog positions of the moon for each day of the year. Mason also made improvements on some of Greenwich's astronomical instruments. Another employee at Greenwich was Jeremiah Dixon, a mathematical genius who invented several astronomical instruments.

In late 1762, Thomas Penn, proprietor of Pennsylvania, and Frederick Calvert, the Sixth Lord Baltimore and proprietor of Maryland, agreed on a boundary. It would start 15 miles from the southernmost tip of the city of Philadelphia and run directly westward. The two proprietors also agreed that the survey would be made by the best engineers in England—Mason and Dixon.

A contract was drawn up on July 20, 1763, spelling out the duties of the surveyors and what they were to be paid: ten shillings six pence a day until their arrival in America, then one pound one shilling daily until they finished the survey. The expenses would be shared equally by the Penn and Calvert families.

Starting the First Scientific Land Survey

Mason and Dixon arrived in America on November 15, 1763, and went right to work to find the starting point of the survey. The southernmost tip of Philadelphia turned out to be the north wall of a house on the south side of Cedar Street, occupied by Thomas Plumstead and Joseph Huddle. It is now 30 South Street. The surveyors decided that if they measured directly south from there, they would end up in the Delaware River, so they traveled directly west for 31 miles.

Here, near John Harland's farmhouse in Newlin Township, Chester County, they erected the first astronomical observatory in Pennsylvania. They used the observatory to take measurements from various stars in order to fix the exact spot from which to start measuring the Pennsylvania-Maryland boundary. Later a stone known as the Stargazers' Stone was set up about 800 feet north of the old observatory.

From a point next to the Stargazers' Stone, Mason and Dixon headed "nearly" 15 miles directly southward to a "Mr. Bryan's field" in Newark, Delaware, a spot that is three miles east of where the Pennsylvania-Maryland border would begin. The engineers pounded a post into the ground to mark the spot where their survey of the border began.

The Only Curved Boundary in the World

For the rest of the summer, Mason and Dixon worked on the "Delaware Circle," the arc-shaped boundary between Delaware and Pennsylvania. They started at the court house in New Castle, Delaware, and measured a

12-mile radius northward to an island in the Delaware River. From there they surveyed the circular line a distance of about 15 miles to where it intersected with the east-west Maryland-Pennsylvania border. The Delaware Circle is the only arc-shaped boundary of a state or country in the world.

On April 4, 1765, Mason and Dixon returned to Bryan's farm, set a zero milestone into the ground, which they designated "Post Marked West," and started surveying the Pennsylvania-Maryland border westward. Their crew consisted of about 40 men. Most were laborers who hacked down trees to clear a 10- to 20-foot-wide swath so the surveyors could have a clear sight-path to the rod man, and the chain carriers could make their measurements.

After four years, Mason and Dixon reached the mouth of Dunkard Creek, in present-day Greene County, about 30 miles east of what is now Pennsylvania's southwest corner. Here the Shawnee Indian war parties warned that they would attack the crew if it went any further. The Englishmen took their final measurement and noted that they had tra- versed "233 miles, 3 chains, and 38 links from the Post mark'd West." Winter came early to the mountains of western Pennsylvania that year, forcing Mason, Dixon, and their crew to trudge eastward through deep snow. It was impossible to transport the remaining limestone markers to western Pennsylvania, so they built mounds of earth to mark the bound- ary every mile.

HOW SURVEYING WAS DONE IN THE 1760s

The surveyor used a sextant, a telescope with cross hairs in the lens that was mounted on a circular metal base with numbers ranging from 1 to 360 degrees (directly north). Charles Mason and Jeremiah Dixon set their sextant at 270 degrees, directly west. The sextant sits on a tripod with a plumb-line hanging down directly over a stake in the ground.

One member of the surveying team, the chain man, took a 66-foot-long chain with a loop on each end and put one loop around the stake in the ground and walked westward to the end of the chain. Accompanying him was the rod man, who carried a pole with an *x* marked on it at the same height as the height of the sextant on the tripod. The rod man placed the pole through the round link at the free end of the chain on the ground.

Up range, the surveyor sighted through his sextant, positioning the lens' cross hairs on the pole. Using hand signals, he told the rod man to move left or right until both cross hairs were lined up. Then he yelled or signaled "Mark" or "Set," which told the rod man to put a stake in the ground where the rod stood. The surveyor's assistant had a portable stand nearby with a map on which he kept a record of every move. When the mark was set, the assistant recorded it, and the team moved forward to the next stake in the ground. When they did this 80 times, they had traversed one mile and they placed a stone marker.

The last job for Mason and Dixon was to make a map of the border for an engraver, and give to Penn and Calvert the length of a degree of longitude along the "West Line," or the border with what would become Ohio. They completed this task and prepared to go home. On September 11, 1768, just two months shy of five years after their arrival, the pair sailed from New York for England. In London two months later, they submitted their final bill for £3,512/9 s; they were promptly paid.

THE BOUNDARY STONES

The Stargazers' Stone was erected to denote the site where Mason and Dixon made observations and measurements to determine the exact spot on earth from which to start their survey of the Pennsylvania-Maryland boundary. To protect it from farmers' equipment and careless drivers, the stone is surrounded by a neat stone wall and is reached by a short flight of steps built into the shoulder of Chester County Road 15032, a few hundred feet north of Pennsylvania Route 162 near Embreeville.

As Mason and Dixon were surveying the border, they erected limestone markers every mile. Each stone was three and a half to five feet long and a foot square. Cut in England, they had the letter *P* engraved on one side and *M* on the other. Every five miles they set a "Crown Stone," bearing the coats of arms of the Penn and Calvert families. Over the years, many of these stones were removed by developers and lost; others were plowed under or badly damaged by farmers' plows. In 1991, the Pennsylvania Society of Land Surveyors began to locate and replace every stone that Mason and Dixon had laid.

There are no memorials to either man in this country, except for the boundary that bears their name—the Mason-Dixon Line. Throughout U.S. history, this line has had the notorious distinction of being the dividing line between slave states and free states, between the Union and the Confederacy in the Civil War, and between the northern, or Yankee, states and the southern states.

During the early 1750s, the French decided to stake their claim to middle America by burying plates in the ground from New York to Virginia. Governor Robert Dinwiddie sent 21-year-old Major George Washington to Fort LeBoeuf, near present-day Erie, in 1753 to ask the French to leave. They refused. Washington returned to Williamsburg, Virginia, to inform the governor, and the British colonies prepared to push out the French with military force.

Governor Dinwiddie promoted Washington to colonel in the Virginia militia and sent him back to western Pennsylvania to build a fort at the confluence of the Monongahela, Allegheny, and Ohio Rivers. Washington sent an advance party to start construction of Fort Prince George, named in honor of the future king, George III. No sooner had the workers arrived than French troops and their Indian allies swooped down and captured the 41 Englishmen. They were released on the condition that they return to Virginia. The French finished construction of the fort and called it Duquesne.

Meanwhile, Colonel Washington and his men entered Pennsylvania, arriving at Great Meadows in present-day Fayette County. An Indian scout ran into the camp and reported sighting a small group of French troops on Chestnut Ridge. Washington led a patrol of about 40 men to the French encampment commanded by Coulon de Jumonville. The Virginians attacked, killing Jumonville and eight others, then taking 21 prisoners. One escaped. Word reached London and Paris, and war broke out between Great Britain and France, raging from America to Europe.

The First (and Only) Time Washington Surrendered

Washington and his men returned to Great Meadows and erected a makeshift stockade called Fort Necessity. The escaped Frenchman made it to Fort Duquesne and alerted his comrades; soon 1,000 French soldiers surrounded Fort Necessity. Washington realized his 140 men did not stand a

Reenactors re-create the Battle of Fort Necessity, which took place on July 3, 1754, near Uniontown. This French and Indian War skirmish marked the only time George Washington ever surrendered.

chance so, on July 3, 1754, he surrendered. Instead of taking prisoners, Coulon de Villiers, the French commander, allowed Washington and his men to return home. This was the only time in his career that Washington ever surrendered.

A few weeks later, Washington returned to Pennsylvania as an aide to General Edward Braddock. One of their scouts was a Berks Countian named Daniel Boone. A few miles from Fort Duquesne, the English army was ambushed by a contingent of French and Indian troops. Washington had several horses shot out from under him, Braddock was mortally wounded, and the British were forced to retreat back to Virginia.

Eventually another campaign was launched against the French, and Fort Duquesne surrendered. It was renamed in honor of British prime minister William Pitt, and is now the city of Pittsburgh.

☞ *To Visit: Fort Necessity National Battlefield*

Today, a replica of Fort Necessity stands 11 miles east of Uniontown on U.S. Route 40. Designated a National Battlefield, it is operated by the National Park Service and is open for visitors.

Fort Necessity National Battlefield
1 Washington Parkway
Farmington, PA 15437
724-329-5512
www.nps.gov/fone
Hours: Daily, 8:30 A.M.-6:30 P.M.
Admission free.

Industry and Business

THE FIRST BREWERY

Most of Pennsylvania's first settlers, particularly the Swedes, avoided drinking water, believing it caused malaria and other diseases. They preferred "comfortable drinks," both fermented and distilled. Foaming pitchers of home-brewed beer were served at almost every meal. Nearly every Swedish farm, dating back to 1645, had a malt house for brewing "small beer," made from hops, ginger, straw, and molasses.

William Penn was fond of beer and, in 1683, had a 20 by 35-foot brew house built at Pennsbury, his estate in Bucks County. Two years later, a friend of Penn's, William Frampton, started the first commer-

William Penn had his own private brewery, which was located in one of the outbuildings (at the right) on his estate, Pennsbury, near Morrisville. This view shows the front of the house, facing the Delaware River. *Courtesy of the Pennsylvania Historical and Museum Commission*

cial brewery in the commonwealth near Front and Dock Streets in Philadelphia. Frampton died the following year and his son continued the business.

GLASS

The first glass factory in western Pennsylvania was established in 1794 by a partnership that included Abraham Alfonse Albert Gallatin, who went on to become President Thomas Jefferson's treasury secretary. The glass plant was built along the Monongahela River about seven miles north of the West Virginia border at present-day New Geneva, Fayette County. Its furnace was heated by wood and had eight windows for making the glass. The firm's name, Gallatin & Company, was later changed to the New Geneva Glass Works.

Plate glass was first produced on a large scale in 1883 by the New York City Plate Glass Company in Creighton, Allegheny County. A few months later the firm changed its name to the Pittsburgh Plate Glass Company.

America's first glass crystal chandelier was cut by William Peter Eichbaum at Bakewell's Glass Works in Pittsburgh in 1810. It consisted of "six lights and shower upon shower of rainbow casting prisms," and was sold for $300 to a Mr. Kerr, who hung it in his hotel.

Record-Making Feats of Glass

Jules Quertimont of Jeannette, Westmoreland County, once blew a "ball" of glass so big that, when flattened, it made a window pane five feet by six feet, one-eighth of an inch thick—said to have been a world's record.

The main ingredient for making glass is silica, a fine white sand that is mixed at a very high temperature. The sand for the 200-inch telescope mirror at the Hale Observatory on Mount Palomar in California came from Mapleton Depot in Huntingdon County. The making of this 40,000-pound, 26-inch-thick mirror took almost the entire year of 1934, and was the most spectacular "casting" done to that time in the field of glass manufacture.

IRON

Pennsylvania was one of the last colonies to get into the iron-making business, but by 1790, the commonwealth was producing half the country's supply of iron. In 1716, Thomas Rutter, onetime bailiff of Germantown, built the Poole bloomery forge on Manatawny Creek in Berks County. This was the first successful ironworks in Pennsylvania. The word *bloomery* is derived from the Anglo-Saxon *bloma*—or "lump." Rutter's forge made blooms, or lumps, that iron workers hammered into bars of pig iron that were sold to craftsmen who specialized in making iron products.

Pig Iron

Early iron furnaces like Rutter's were stone chimneys, shaped roughly like a pyramid, usually about 25 feet high and about 25 feet wide at the base. A wooden ramp was built from a hill out to the top of the forge. Workmen wheeled barrows of charcoal out to the top of the forge and dumped it in. Next, limestone and iron ore were dumped on top of the charcoal. Below, another workman started a wood fire (later coal replaced the wood). When the charcoal was heated, it melted the limestone and iron ore. The limestone absorbed the impurities from the iron ore and floated to the top. The purified iron, or refined iron, trickled to the bottom as a liquid and was drawn off into troughs or ruts dug into the dirt floor of the forge. These troughs were called "pigs," and the cooled iron was called "pig iron."

The First Ironmistress

Rebecca Webb Pennock was born in 1794 in West Marlborough Township, Chester County. Her father was the ironmaster at the Federal Slitting Mill on Bull Run, about five miles from present-day Coatesville, Chester County. Rebecca attended a girls' boarding school in Wilmington, Delaware, but she also spent a lot of time with her father at his ironworks and learned the iron business.

At 19, Rebecca married Dr. Charles Lukens, who soon gave up medicine to lease the Brandywine Rolling Mill in Coatesville, one of Rebecca's father's ironworks, for $420 a year. Together Rebecca and Charles ran the mill. There they made the first iron plate for the boiler and hull of a naval vessel.

Lukens died in 1825, leaving the mill in poor shape financially, as well as a 31-year-old widow with five children to support and a sixth on the way. Rebecca's father had died before her husband, leaving everything to his wife. When Rebecca decided to run the mill on her own, her mother disapproved and never offered any support. Nevertheless, Rebecca took charge of the mill and soon built up its production to 500 tons a year. Rebecca Lukens was the first woman in the country to run an iron-making business, and perhaps the first to be involved in heavy industry.

Rebecca Lukens died in 1854 at the age of 60. Five years later, her mill in Coatesville was renamed Lukens Steel. It is now the oldest steel manufacturing firm in the country.

WOMAN UNDERTAKER

Nellie Sweeny Hayes was one of the first women in Pennsylvania to earn a license as an undertaker. Her father, John Sweeny, was one of the first undertakers in the state to be licensed and went on to become one of the oldest active morticians in the country.

Nellie Sweeny was a member of Houtzdale High School's first graduating class, the class of 1891. She then attended Lock Haven Normal School, now Lock Haven University. In 1917, she married Morgan Hayes, who ran a garage in Houtzdale, Clearfield County.

The Sweeny-Hayes business on Hannah Street in Houtzdale was a combination funeral parlor and furniture store. This was only natural in those days because undertakers usually made their own coffins. The income from furniture sales helped when the undertaking business was slow.

Nellie Sweeny Hayes died on June 2, 1958. She never revealed her age.

FEMALE JOURNALIST

Anne Newport Royall was a pioneer female journalist in Washington, D.C., and one of the first women newspaper editors in the country.

Born Anne Newport on June 11, 1769, in Baltimore, Maryland, she moved to Westmoreland County, Pennsylvania, as a youngster. After her father was killed in a battle with Indians, Anne and her widowed mother walked all the way to Virginia, where they became servants in the household of a Revolutionary War veteran named Major William Royall. The major encouraged Anne to read and she soon developed a talent as a writer. Eventually Anne and Major Royall got married, and when Royall died, Anne inherited the major's estate. A few years later, another heir came forward and challenged Anne's claim. Litigation lasted several more years, and when it was all over, Anne had lost not only the case, but any means of income as well.

Anne suffered another loss. Her husband had received a pension for serving in the Revolutionary War, but when he died, the pension payments stopped because the federal government's policy did not include pension payments to a veteran's widow. Anne went to Washington and lobbied Congress to grant a pension to the widows of Revolutionary War veterans. The issue was debated for a quarter century, during which time Anne traveled and wrote travelogues for subscribers all over the country. After criticizing politicians in her writings, she was arrested and convicted as a "common scold." The penalty was only a $10 fine, but her reputation was tarnished and readers dropped their subscriptions.

Anne returned to the nation's capital and started a newspaper called *Paul Pry*, which debuted on December 3, 1831. In it she lashed out at anybody in authority she believed was corrupt and pressed for the dismissal or defeat of dishonest officials and politicians. Anne also wrote against bank monopolies and championed tolerance for Roman Catholics and immigrants. As if all that were not enough, she published a literary magazine, *Huntress*, for 18 years.

Finally, the pension bill was passed by Congress. Anne received $1,200, but after she paid her bills, she was left with a paltry $10.

Anne Royall died on October 1, 1854, and was buried in an unmarked grave in the National Congressional Cemetery. Her crusading spirit against corruption and greed has earned her the distinction of being the "Grandmother of all Muckrakers."

THE FOUNDERS OF A PHARMACEUTICAL FIRM

In the mid-1800s, Sylvester Johnson, a cattle farmer in Carbondale, Lackawanna County, had three sons who all went into different professions: James became a civil engineer; Edward, an attorney; and Robert went to Poughkeepsie, New York, at the age of 16 as an apprentice in an apothecary shop. There he learned how to mix medicated plasters, ointments, and tinctures.

On completing his apprenticeship, Robert moved to New York City and started a wholesale drug and brokerage business. In 1874, he became a junior partner in the Brooklyn firm of Seabury & Johnson, which manufactured pharmaceutical preparations. Their first big product was a new kind of bandage made with a rubber base and a sticking plaster made of silk with isinglass (a type of gelatin). This was the forerunner of the Band-Aid, which would be developed by Johnson & Johnson a half century later.

A turning point for Robert came when, at the age of 31, he attended the 1876 Medical Congress in Philadelphia. The main speaker was the famous British surgeon Sir Joseph Lister, whose topic was the future of pharmaceuticals. Robert was fascinated by Lister's remarks about sterilizing surgical bandages in carbolic acid.

At the time, business was going so well for Seabury & Johnson that the firm had moved to larger quarters in East Orange, New Jersey. Robert wasted no time in convincing his brothers to join his company. James, the engineer of the family, began to design machinery to produce modern antiseptic dressings (bandages). Edward, the attorney, discovered he had hidden talents for marketing and advertising.

Johnson & Johnson

Within five years, James and Edward left their brother's company and, with only a thousand dollars of capital, they organized their own company, Johnson & Johnson, in New Brunswick, New Jersey.

Robert Wood Johnson was not part of the original Johnson & Johnson because he was still tied in with Seabury & Johnson. In July 1885, he sold his half interest, promising that he would not do business "of like character" for 10 years. But it turned out that he was released from that restriction in just a few years.

In 1886, Robert joined his brothers in a new corporation to "manufacture and market medical, pharmaceutical, surgical, and antiseptic specialties." They brought Listerism, the use of antiseptics in surgery, to the United States. They were also the first to develop catgut sutures for use in surgery. And before the turn of the century, they created the first zinc oxide adhesive plaster.

Edward, the minority partner, left the company in 1899 and started Mead Johnson & Company (his middle name was Mead) to make dietary and baby foods, vitamins, and, later, pharmaceuticals.

That's how three brothers from Carbondale, Pennsylvania, became the world's biggest names in the pharmaceutical business.

THE FIRST CREMATORY

Dr. F. Julius LeMoyne was 77 years old and still practicing medicine in 1875 in the borough of Washington, near the southwestern corner of Pennsylvania. At the time, cremation had been introduced in Europe, and

The LeMoyne Crematory, the first crematory, stands today at South Main Street Extension in Washington, Pennsylvania. *Courtesy of the Washington County Historical Society, Washington, PA*

the doctor made a study of both the arguments for the practice and the various types of furnaces in use. He designed his own gas-fired cremation furnace and, in 1875, started to build the first crematory in the United States, and a structure to house it, on his own property—at the top of a hill just outside town known as Gallows Hill.

As soon as word of the project got out, sightseers came from other states to watch the construction. Even President Grant came from Washington, D.C., to see it, and minstrel comedians found ways of working LeMoyne's crematory into their acts.

LeMoyne had his first customer in December 1876. Joseph Henry Louis, Baron de Palm, holder of an armload of royal titles including Chamberlain of His Majesty the King of Bavaria, died while visiting the United States. According to his will, he directed his executors to have his body cremated, so they brought the corpse to Washington, Pennsylvania, trailed by doctors, over 40 newspaper reporters from across the country, and devotees of all things macabre.

LeMoyne met with hundreds of curiosity-seekers and newsfolk in the town hall and answered their questions. The baron's executor, Colonel Olcott, gave a eulogy for the deceased. Then the casket was placed in a hearse and made its way to Gallows Hill, followed by a large throng. Baron de Palm became the first person cremated in the United States.

On December 13, the New York *Daily Graphic* carried a full page of pictures of the cremation "from sketches by our special artists and photographs by Messrs. Rithwell and Rogers, Washington, Pennsylvania." The pictures show a team of horses struggling up the steep incline of Gallows Hill, pulling the hearse, plus a bevy of dignitaries that included George P. Hayes, president of Washington and Jefferson College.

LeMoyne was deluged with requests for interviews and invitations to address public meetings. Now 78 years old, he could not take the strain, so he put his thoughts on the history and benefits of cremation, and detailed descriptions of the furnace and the cremation process, into a 20-page pamphlet, which was sold everywhere. It led to the establishment of new crematories in the United States and the widespread adoption of the practice.

Less than three years later, on October 4, 1879, LeMoyne died and was cremated in the furnace he had built. The last cremation there took place in 1900, but the LeMoyne Crematory still stands today at South Main Street Extension, Washington, Pennsylvania.

OUR COUNTRY'S FIRST LABOR UNIONS

Pennsylvania is the birthplace of labor unions in the United States. During the colonial days of the early 1700s, skilled craftsmen found it advantageous to form guilds for the purpose of trading information and determining prices. Guilds were forerunners of unions. One such guild, the Carpenters' Company of Philadelphia, was organized in 1724, and in 1770 started to build Carpenters' Hall, where the First Continental Congress convened in 1774. The first labor associations were organized by workers in specific crafts to protect their members from being replaced by machines or immigrant workers.

The first permanent trade union was organized in 1794 by the cordwainers (shoemakers) of Philadelphia. The shoe workers of Pittsburgh soon followed suit. In 1825, carpenters in Boston went on strike, demanding a 10-hour day. Pennsylvania workingmen joined their cause. This culminated in 1827 with the formation of the Mechanics Union of Trade Associations, which, for the first time in American history, combined several unions in different trades under one organization. A year later, the association wielded its political clout by starting the Working Men's Party, the first labor party in the world. The party published the *Mechanics' Free Press* in Philadelphia from 1828 to 1831, the first labor journal in the world.

The next step in unionism, a nationwide organization, originated in Pennsylvania with the formation in 1859 of the National Union of Machinists and Blacksmiths and the Molders' International Union. The leader of this movement was William Sylvis of Armagh, Indiana County.

The First Modern Labor Union

The Noble Order of the Knights of Labor (K of L) began in Philadelphia in 1869 as a secret society of tailors led by Uriah Stephens. Shortly thereafter it opened its doors to other tradesmen, and when the depression of 1873 forced many unions out of business, the miners of western Pennsylvania joined, as did the Pittsburgh railroad workers after their unsuccessful strike of 1877. The Pittsburgh chapter, now strengthened by the miners' and trainmen's memberships, challenged Philadelphia for leadership of the K of L. The Pittsburgh and Philadelphia rivals met in Reading, Berks County, in 1878 and agreed to establish the Knights of Labor as a nation-wide labor union. Its leader for the next 14 years was Terrence V. Powderly. Afterwards, Powderly served three terms as mayor of Scranton, Lackawanna County.

The K of L grew to 700,000 members: men and women, whites and African Americans. (Barred from membership were bankers, lawyers, gamblers, and liquor dealers.) But the union declined quite suddenly after the "eight-hour day" strike, which climaxed in Chicago on May 4, 1886, when 10 people died and 50 were injured in the Haymarket Riot.

But that was hardly the end of the labor union movement in Pennsylvania. As the Knights of Labor was shrinking, the American Federation of Labor, organized in Pittsburgh on November 15, 1881, was growing. It remains one of the strongest unions in the world as part of the AFL-CIO.

WHEN COAL WAS KING (AND MINERS WERE SERFS)

Pennsylvania was the country's biggest coal producer—anthracite and bituminous—from the early 1800s to the mid-1900s. The mine owners watched the coal going out and the money coming in, all the while casting a near-blind eye to the deplorable conditions of their miners. The owners were rich princes, and their miners serfs who worked 12 to 16 hours a day in an unsafe, unhealthy, underground cocoon. For his labor a miner got $10 a week—plus a bill for his tools, dynamite, and work clothes. Anyone who complained was fired; strikers were fined, then fired. Instead of sick leave and medical insurance, a miner usually got asthma, pneumonia, or heart disease. Something had to change, but several attempts to unionize America's mine workers ended in futility.

The first miners union to take hold was the Workingmen's Benevolent Association, founded in 1868 in the anthracite town of St. Clair, Schuylkill County. Its leader was an Irish immigrant named John Siney. His main adversary was Frank Gowen, kingpin of the Philadelphia and Reading Railroad, who accused union members of being part of the Irish terrorist group known as the Molly Maguires.

Siney took his struggle nationwide by organizing coal miners into the Miners National Association of the United States in 1873. He presided over it until the "Big Strike of 1875," which shut down mines in Pennsylvania, Ohio, and West Virginia. When the soot and coal dust cleared, the mine owners were the victors, and the union collapsed. The ordeal brought on the untimely death of Siney at the age of 49. He was buried beneath an impressive monument in St. Mary's Cemetery in St. Clair.

Twenty years later, John Mitchell took on Siney's cause when he organized the large and powerful United Mine Workers.

Paving Pennsylvania

THE FIRST ROADS

When white men first arrived in Pennsylvania, they found the land crisscrossed by a maze of roads and trails stretching in every direction. The Indians used the first paths by following trails made by deer and other wild animals. Later, the white settlers built roads over these old Indian trails.

Probably the first vehicular road in the commonwealth was built by the Dutch in 1660 from Kingston, New York, to their copper mines near present-day Stroudsburg, Monroe County. After the British took over New Netherland in 1664, the Duke of York ordered this road extended to the Dutch and Swedish settlement at the site of Philadelphia. Designated a "King's Highway," it ran through Morrisville and Bristol.

FIRST PUBLIC ROADS

The first public roads were located in Oxford Township, Philadelphia County. The courses and distances of two such roads were mentioned in the records of the Provincial Council of October 31, 1696.

An act of 1700 authorized more king's highways, with trees and brush cut to a width of 50 feet. A royal road was opened from Philadelphia to

Chester in 1706. Five years later came the Old York Road, which passed through Jenkintown, Willow Grove, Hatboro, Furlong, and Buckingham to New Hope, Bucks County. In 1722, a road branched off the Old York and extended to Doylestown and Easton. About 200 years later, this became U.S. Route 611.

The real beginning of Pennsylvania's system of highways was on January 29, 1731, when the citizens of Lancaster petitioned the Provincial Council: "Not having the conveniency of any navigable water to bring the produce of the laborers to Philadelphia...becomes the want of suitable roads for carriages to pass." Two years later the council approved funds for the road (which took another eight years to complete). This 62-mile-long road, called the Great Conestoga Road, was the start of the Pennsylvania Road, which eventually ran from Philadelphia to Pittsburgh.

THE FIRST TURNPIKE IN THE UNITED STATES

The province, and later the state, of Pennsylvania could not afford to spend much money to maintain the Pennsylvania Road. By late 1791, the road was used so much that its dirt surface was ground into powder. When it rained, this powder turned to a soupy muck and rendered the road impassable.

On April 9, 1792, the state legislature voted to permit the governor to incorporate a company to rebuild and widen the road from Philadelphia to Lancaster. Surveyors went to work immediately to lay out a road with a minimum 50-foot right-of-way. Rock breakers used sledge hammers to smash limestone into pieces small enough to pass through a seven-inch metal hoop for the road base and a three-inch one for the basic layer. This process was called "macadam" after its inventor, John Loudon McAdam, a Scotsman. Completed in 1795, the turnpike cost $464,142.41, or about $7,141 per mile. It was the first macadamized road in the United States.

The Lancaster Turnpike, as it was called, was so named because every 15 miles or so, drovers and riders had to pay a toll. At each toll point, a long pole, or pike, blocked the road. The pike was about 60 feet long and mounted on a tree stump at the edge of the road. Fifty feet hung over the road, and a huge spike held the pike to the stump. The 10-foot length that extended off the road had slabs of iron nailed to it to act as a balancing counterweight. Whenever a traveler paid his or her toll, the tolltaker or his helper pushed or turned the pike to let the traveler pass. Hence the name "turnpike."

In 1794, another turnpike company, the Lancaster and Susquehanna, extended the road westward to Columbia, Lancaster County. Over the years, the Lancaster Turnpike was improved, paved, widened for motor vehicles, and called the Lincoln Highway. Today it roughly follows U.S. Route 30.

THE FIRST ROAD IN WESTERN PENNSYLVANIA

George Washington had a hand in planning the first road over the Allegheny Mountains. In 1753, Governor Dinwiddie of Virginia sent a young Major Washington to Fort LeBoeuf, in present-day Erie County, to deliver the king's demand that the French leave the territory. Washington sailed up the Potomac River to Fort Cumberland, Maryland. From there he trekked overland, guided by Christopher Gist. They followed what was then known as Nemacolin's Path, named after the well-known Delaware scout who had blazed it many years earlier. The path led to the confluence of the Allegheny, Monongahela, and Ohio Rivers, now known as the Golden Triangle of Pittsburgh.

Gist and Washington then floated up the Allegheny to Fort LeBoeuf and gave the king's letter to the French commander, Captain Jacques Legardeur. The French refused to leave Pennsylvania and soon the colonies were embroiled in the French and Indian War. To bolster their defense of the frontier, the French built Fort Duquesne at present-day Pittsburgh.

Braddock's Road

The king appointed General Edward Braddock as commander of British forces in America with the mission of defeating the French. Braddock's strategy was to march on Fort Duquesne and reduce it to ashes. On March 15, 1755, Robert Hunter Morris, governor of the Province of Pennsylvania, addressed the Pennsylvania Assembly, stating that the colony had been tasked by the Crown to furnish supplies for the army and build a road to carry them. The new road roughly followed the trail blazed by Washington two years earlier.

The job would be done by 300 men from the Cumberland Valley and from Lancaster and York Counties, along with a detachment of another 300 soldiers, commanded by Major Russell Chapman. They started at Cumberland, Maryland, on May 30, 1755, and proceeded in a northwest-erly direction across the colony line into the Laurel Highlands of Pennsylvania. Using only hand tools, they broadened a foot trail into a wagon road 12 feet wide. Progress was painfully slow—from two to five miles a day. Streams had to be bridged and swamps had to be filled with logs and dirt to be made passable. To cross the steep mountains, the road zig-zagged up and down the sides. Between June 7 and 10, the army began to march in three divisions. The road was so narrow that the wagons were strung out over a distance of four miles. It took the army two months to traverse the 115 miles of mountain wilderness. Among the troops were George Washington and Daniel Boone.

Finally, on July 9, the 1,200 soldiers of the advance reached a spot near the Monongahela River, about 10 miles from Fort Duquesne. Suddenly some 800 Indians and French ambushed the tired British and their colonial militia, and two-thirds of them were killed or wounded. Washington had three horses shot out from under him; Braddock was wounded and died four days later. The survivors retreated back to Fort Cumberland.

Today, the site of that ambush is a town named after the general— Braddock, Pennsylvania. The spot where the fighting was most intense became a steel mill owned by Andrew Carnegie. And what became of Braddock's road? It hit the big time!

FIRST FEDERALLY PLANNED AND FUNDED HIGHWAY

Albert Gallatin was born to aristocracy in Geneva, Switzerland, where he received a liberal education. He immigrated to America in 1780 and became a land speculator in the backwoods of western Pennsylvania. He built a mansion called Friendship Hill in 1789 near Point Marion in Fayette County and was elected to the U.S. Senate in 1794. He represented western Pennsylvania in Congress until President Thomas Jefferson appointed him secretary of the Treasury in 1801. At the request of the U.S. Senate, Gallatin presented a report "respecting roads and canals" on April 4, 1808. This became the basis of the country's transportation policies for the next decade.

Gallatin's report promoted three concepts: First, the federal government should finance transportation projects including highways and canals of national importance. Second, those routes should be constructed that would yield reasonable returns on the original investment. Third, a nationwide transportation system was essential to the national defense.

The National Road

On March 29, 1806, Congress passed the "Act to Regulate the Laying Out and Making a Road from Cumberland in the State of Maryland, to the State of Ohio." Due to Gallatin's influence, the National Road, as it was called, would pass through western Pennsylvania. (Even then, politicking could affect the exact route of the new road!) Property owners were eager to donate 65-foot right-of-way strips through their farms because of the expected increase in the value of their property and the availability of new jobs.

The government appointed three commissioners, a surveyor, two chainmen, and one marker. The surveyor earned two dollars a day while the chainmen and marker each received a dollar per day plus expenses. They laid out a route that roughly followed Braddock's road. Between 1806 and 1808, the team marked out a 131-mile route from Cumberland, Maryland, through Uniontown, Brownsville, and Washington, Pennsylvania, to Wheeling, West Virginia, where the road would connect with Zanes' Trace in Ohio.

Work on the National Road commenced in 1811 at an initial cost of $6,000 per mile. Thousands of men were hired to fell trees, dig out stumps, and clear underbrush. Hundreds of wagons hauled in equipment and carried away refuse. Hills were leveled; crews of men with picks and shovels prepared the roadbed. Just as with the Lancaster Turnpike, the National Road was macadamized with a base of heavy stone topped with gravel or fine stone and dirt.

Construction was completed to Wheeling, West Virginia, by 1818, and eventually reached Valdalia, Illinois. Soon it was the main route to the country's western frontier. Along the way there were inns about 20 miles apart where stagecoaches and wagon trains could stop for the night.

The National Road was known by many names: Great Cumberland Road, National Pike, Old Pike, Ohio Road, Uncle Sam's Highways, Great Western Turnpike, United States Road, or just The Road.

BRIDLE BELLS

The freight trucks of the 18th century and the early 19th century were Conestoga wagons, usually driven by six horses whose bridles were adorned with dozens of bells. At times, a wagon would break down because of a broken axle or a loose wheel, and the drover would seek out a passer-by to help him fix his wagon. As a reward, the person who helped was given one of the bells, which the drover took off his horses' bridle. By the time the wagon reached its destination, there would often be few or no bells left on the bridle. This gave rise to the American expression "I'll be there with bells on," meaning I plan to have a safe, uneventful trip.

By 1829, Congress had spent $100,000 to overhaul the road in Pennsylvania. As soon as the job was done, the feds turned over jurisdiction and maintenance of the road to the states through which it passed.

Pay a Toll

To raise money for maintenance, the states erected tollhouses to collect fares. These tollhouses were placed about 15 miles apart. Most were erected to resemble a lighthouse. The toll rates of those times were listed on a large board on the tollhouse building. A wagon was charged by the size of its wheels and the number of animals pulling it. When livestock was herded along the road, the drovers were charged 6 cents per 20 sheep or pigs; cattle cost 12 cents per 20. Sometimes a teamster or rider on horseback would try to avoid paying the toll by going around the tollhouse. The tollkeeper, wise to this ruse, posted a lookout on the upper floor of the tollhouse. Once alerted, the tollkeeper would ride out after the scofflaw and slap him with a fine of three dollars, which was expensive—quite a bit more than the eight-cent toll he would have paid for a horse and rider.

There were six tollhouses in Pennsylvania along the National Road. One, near Addison, Somerset County, still stands and is privately owned; and another, near Farmington, Fayette County, was constructed of stone. The other four—Searights, near Uniontown, Fayette County, one near Beallsville, one slightly east of Washington, and one just to the east of West Alexander, all of Washington County—were constructed of brick. These houses also served as the home of the tollkeeper and his family.

Searights Tollhouse

Built in 1835, Searights Tollhouse is now a registered National Historic Landmark and is at times open to the public as a museum and information center. Owned by the Pennsylvania Historical and Museum Commission, the restored structure has three rooms and is managed by the Fayette County Historical Society. It received its name from the nearby village of

Searights Tollhouse in Fayette County is a registered National Historic Landmark. It was named after the nearby village of Searights, which was named in honor of William Searight, owner of a tavern on the National Road. *Courtesy of the Pennsylvania Historical and Museum Commission*

Searights, which was named after its most renowned citizen, William Searight. Searight owned a busy tavern on the National Road, of which he had been a contractor. Later he was appointed commissioner of the Pennsylvania section, but seems to have had no connection to the toll-house itself.

☞ To Visit: Searights Tollhouse

Searights Tollhouse
Fayette County Historical Society
P.O. Box 193
Uniontown, PA 15401
412-439-4422
Hours: Memorial Day through mid-October: Tuesday-Saturday, 10 A.M.-4 P.M.; Sunday, 2-6 P.M.
Admission charged.

THE FIRST IRON BRIDGE IN THE UNITED STATES

There were a succession of bridges along the National Road. One crossed over Dunlap's Creek in Brownsville, Fayette County—a chain bridge of the type invented by James Finley. It stood 20 to 30 feet above the creek, but one day in 1820 it came crashing down because of the weight of snow. The federal government appropriated funds to reconstruct the road in 1832, and placed Captain Richard Delafield of the Army Corps of Engineers in charge of the project. Delafield decided to replace the chain bridge with an iron span; iron foundries were nearby at Brownsville, and several cast-iron bridges had already been built in Europe.

The higher-ups in the army were so impressed with the progress that Delafield made on the road that they promoted him to major and appointed him superintendent of the U.S. Military Academy at West Point, New York. Captain George Dutton replaced him on August 8, 1839. On October 15, Dutton wrote to his boss, Colonel Joseph G. Totten, chief of the Army Corps of Engineers in Washington, D.C., that the iron bridge at Main Street in Brownsville was completed and had opened for traffic on July 4, 1839.

The iron foundries in the Brownsville area have long been abandoned, but the country's first iron bridge is still in use. Listed as a National Civil Engineering Landmark, the bridge still has no restrictions on use by any "legal load" truck traffic.

THE FIRST SUPERHIGHWAY TOLL ROAD

On the night of September 30, 1940, in Cumberland County, automobiles began to line up at the Carlisle toll booth that stood on the eastern end of the new Pennsylvania Turnpike. By midnight there were about 40 cars in line, waiting to be the first to ride on the new superhighway. At 12:01 A.M. on October 1, the turnpike opened and the first car through the gate was driven by Homer D. Romberger of Carlisle. Coincidentally, he had also witnessed the ceremonial turning of the first spade of dirt to start construction only 23 months earlier at a spot 10 miles to the west. But in reality, construction of the turnpike, which was to be the forerunner of the interstate highway system, had begun a half century earlier.

Magnates and Monopolies

During the 1870s, there were no governmental price controls or any other federal interference with American business. Companies competed with each other in the spirit of free enterprise—meaning that they were free to engage in throat-cutting, back-stabbing, and manipulating each other into bankruptcy. Smaller companies without enough capital to survive the price wars were usually bought out by larger companies. In this manner, John D. Rockefeller was monopolizing the oil industry, Andrew Carnegie was controlling the steel industry, and William Henry Vanderbilt was building his own empire in railroads.

After succeeding his father as president of the New York Central Railroad, Vanderbilt turned his attention toward Pennsylvania and his main rival there, the Pennsylvania Railroad. In 1883, Vanderbilt formed a syndicate with Frank Gowen, president of the Reading Railroad, and steel magnates Andrew Carnegie, Henry Oliver, Henry C. Phipps, Henry Clay Frick, and E. M. Ferguson. Each man kicked in over a million dollars to build a shortcut to Pittsburgh.

Vanderbilt's plan was to revive the South Penn Railroad, first surveyed and laid out in 1839–40 by Colonel Charles Schattler of the Army Corps of Engineers. Schattler had actually surveyed two routes across the commonwealth. One roughly followed the old Pennsylvania Canal and became the main line of the Pennsylvania Railroad, completed in 1850. The other was a parallel route along the southern tier of the state, but it was never built. It was along this southern route that the Vanderbilt conglomerate started to build its railroad. The Pennsylvania Railroad meandered up and down mountains and followed the curves of the Juniata and Susquehanna Rivers, but Vanderbilt's South Penn Railroad would cut a straight line through the mountains and deliver steel to New York and the rest of the East Coast faster and cheaper.

Construction started at the Reading terminus in Harrisburg, Dauphin County, and went west to Port Perry on the Monongahela River near Braddock, Allegheny County. Thousands of laborers, stone masons, grinders, and drillers worked along the 209-mile route. They built nine tremendous tunnels, each more than a mile long, through the Allegheny Mountains. These included the tunnels at Sideling Hill, Ray's Hill, Blue Mountain, and Tuscarora Mountain. By September 1885, the South Penn Railroad was 60 percent finished. Six and a half tunnels were excavated; more than five million cubic yards of grading was completed. But 27 men had been killed, mainly in the tunnels by dynamite and cave-ins. Costs were running twice the original estimate, to the tune of $10 million. The investors began to worry.

Finally, 48-year-old John Pierpont Morgan, banker, financier, and all-round wheeler-dealer, stepped into the act. Morgan felt that not only were both the New York Central and Pennsylvania Railroads threatened with bankruptcy over their silly rivalry, but the entire financial structure of the country was about to topple. Using his muscle as a director of the New York Central, Morgan called a peace conference of the Vanderbilt forces and the Pennsy people aboard his yacht.

After much discussion, the rail executives agreed to a truce with these terms: First, both railroads would get out of each other's territory. Second, the New York Central would turn over its unfinished South Penn Railroad to the Pennsy. And third, the Pennsy would turn over its lines in New Jersey to the New York Central.

But the Commonwealth of Pennsylvania didn't like this agreement and filed suit against it. The state supreme court ruled, "Pennsylvania law forbids a railroad to purchase a competing line. Therefore this court orders the Pennsylvania Railroad to cease and desist any work on the South Penn."

Over the next half century, the South Penn right-of-way from Irwin, Westmoreland County, to Harrisburg was overgrown with trees and brush; water filled the floors of the tunnels, which became breeding grounds for bats and vermin. Today, the piers of the South Penn Bridge across the Susquehanna between Harrisburg and New Cumberland, Cumberland County, still stand.

It Started with a Joke

During the 1930s, the South Penn Railroad piers across the Susquehanna could be seen from the office of William Sutherland, general manager of the Pennsylvania Motor Truck Association in Harrisburg. One evening in January 1935, Sutherland was having dinner with Clifford Patterson, a legislator from Washington County, and Victor LeCoq, an employee of the state planning commission. Jokingly, Sutherland quipped, "Cliff, I've been looking at those old South Penn piers and have a great idea for you."

"What's that?" asked the politician.

With a twinkle in his eye, Sutherland replied, "How 'bout getting the state to build a highway over the old railbed for our truckers!"

Intrigued by the wisecrack, Representative Patterson started asking questions. Their discussion went far into the night. When the three men went their separate ways that night, Patterson realized that he had become obsessed with the idea of a superhighway across the commonwealth. This was the beginning of the Pennsylvania Turnpike.

An undertaker from Monongahela, Patterson was new to politics at the time. But having to drive on the winding, narrow roads from his constituency in far western Pennsylvania to Harrisburg, he was fully aware of the inadequacy of the state's highways. And with the growing number of trucks and automobiles, the situation would only get worse. Patterson decided to champion the cause of a new superhighway. To drum up support, Sutherland printed a map of the proposed highway. On the reverse side was the history of the South Penn Railroad over whose railbed the highway would be built.

On April 23, 1935, Patterson introduced a resolution to the Pennsylvania House and Senate to empower Governor George Earle to appoint a commission to study the feasibility of a superhighway across the state. Since a commission would not cost any money, and because they were anxious to adjourn, the legislators quickly approved the resolution. Virtually none of them dreamed it would result in the Pennsylvania Turnpike.

WPA Comes Through

Meanwhile, state and local governments had created public works projects to provide jobs during the Great Depression of the 1930s. A lot of towns got their first sewers, hospitals, and paved streets this way. The money for most of this construction came from the federal Works Progress Administration (WPA), headed by Harry Hopkins, a crony of President Franklin D. Roosevelt's.

At the same time, Warren Van Dyke was Pennsylvania's secretary of highways and a member of the commission to study the feasibility of building a superhighway across the state on an old railroad bed. In July 1935, he applied for a WPA grant to survey the route. Van Dyke's application reached Hopkins, who liked it so much that he brought it to his boss.

With Hitler in power in Germany and Japan at war with China, President Roosevelt foresaw the new highway as a fast way to move troops and equipment in the war that was likely to erupt. Thus the president approved a WPA grant, the first funding for the Pennsylvania Turnpike.

On October 10, 1938, the Reconstruction Finance Corporation purchased $35,000 worth of turnpike bonds and the WPA pledged to finance up to 45 percent of the cost, not to exceed $28.1 million. However, there was a catch—construction of the turnpike had to be finished in less than two years, by June 29, 1940, because the WPA would go out of existence on that day.

The state put out a call for bids on October 14, and the first contract was awarded on October 26 to L. M. Hutchinson, to grade a 10-mile stretch in Cumberland County. The turnpike commissioners also hired the J.E. Greiner engineering firm of Baltimore, Maryland, to design the new highway.

Walter A. Jones, chairman of the turnpike commission, held a little ground-breaking ceremony near Carlisle, Cumberland County, on October 27, 1938. Hardly anyone attended. One who did come was a local woman, Mrs. Eberly, and her eight children. Since no program was arranged, she felt free to make some remarks. "This is the greatest day in the history of our mountain district," exclaimed Mrs. Eberly. "I got my children out of school to be present at this historic occasion!" This was the first inkling the commissioners had of how the public felt about the new highway.

Surveyors began to stake out the turnpike in late October 1938. By the spring of that year, the professional engineers had concluded that some 160 miles of superhighway could be built from Carlisle, in central Pennsylvania, to Irwin, near Pittsburgh, for about $70 million. At the same time, the George Vang Company of Pittsburgh had begun to pump out the water from the old South Penn Railroad tunnels, which would be part of the turnpike.

Breakneck Speed

Commission chairman Walter Jones awarded 155 contracts to 118 different companies and put some 15,000 people to work on the turnpike. Over the next 20 months, he had to contend with lawsuits, jurisdictional strikes between labor unions, and delays from rock slides. Nevertheless, Jones kept the work going.

The right-of-way for the highway would be 200 feet wide, and inclines were limited to not more than 3 percent. Over its entire 160-mile length, the highway would not have a single grade crossing or crossroad. This meant that 299 bridges had to be built over streams and across valleys, and most of the bridges for roads that intersected with the new highway had to be built over the turnpike. Housing was so scarce that some workers lived, with their families, in tents near the construction sites.

The frantic race to lay the roadbed of the Pennsylvania Turnpike before the deadline for completion in 1940. *Courtesy of the Pennsylvania Turnpike Commission*

Then, in the spring of 1940, just three months before the deadline, heavy rains forced almost all work to cease on the highway for the entire month of April. Only four miles of pavement had been laid. By early May, one of the strangest races in the history of road construction got underway. Twenty-nine paving companies with 10,000 men and $4 million worth of equipment worked around the clock to lay concrete. Nearly every contractor broke its past records, and one set a new one by laying heavy concrete roadway, 14 feet wide, at the speed of 125 feet per hour.

Meanwhile, another record-breaking pace was being set in the tunnels. Crews were boring three and a half miles per day through seven mountains. First, one work shift drilled about 100 holes 10 feet deep into the hard rock. Next, they packed explosives into the holes and detonated them. The next shift loaded the rubble on temporary railcars for removal. They enlarged six of the old South Penn Railroad tunnels this way and built a new one at Allegheny Mountain. Buildings to house huge ventilating fans to remove the deadly exhaust fumes were erected at the tunnel portals.

Another type of construction took place alongside the turnpike. To give drivers a break to rest, get fuel, or eat, 10 service plazas were built some 25 to 30 miles apart, at a total cost of $500,000. The buildings at these plazas resembled early Pennsylvania stone houses.

Model for the Future

Construction of the Pennsylvania Turnpike was completed just under the wire. The opening ceremony, however, was postponed so many times that politicians and VIPs got fed up and canceled it altogether. Finally, without any fanfare, the turnpike opened for traffic at 12:01 A.M. on Tuesday, October 1, 1940. That following Sunday, October 6, some 10,000 motorists waited in line up to four hours to pay their tolls and enter the road. From the moment it was completed, the Pennsylvania Turnpike was a success. Trucking companies suddenly discovered that they could nearly double their payloads over the mountains by using the gentle slopes of the turn-

Pennsylvania Turnpike motorists line up at Irwin, waiting for the gates to open at 12:01 A.M., October 1, 1940. *Courtesy of the Pennsylvania Turnpike Commission*

pike. Tourists flocked to the pike not only to enjoy the novelty of riding through its tunnels, but also to find out how fast their cars could go—the turnpike had no speed limit! (A short time later, signs were erected declaring a 50 mph limit, the same as other major state highways.)

THE TURNPIKE'S FIRST TRAFFIC TICKET

An unidentified motorist sneaked on the turnpike the Saturday before it formally opened. He was arrested at the east portal of the Tuscarora tunnel near Chambersburg by Private Henry Lewczyk of the state motor police and charged with "tipsy driving."

One of the very first tollbooths along the Pennsylvania Turnpike in 1940. *Courtesy of the Pennsylvania Turnpike Commission*

Extending the Turnpike

Chairman Jones' plans to extend the turnpike to the Ohio and New Jersey state lines were shelved until after World War II. The second section, from Harrisburg to King of Prussia, Montgomery County, was completed in November 1950. A western extension to the Ohio line opened a year later, and the portion north of Philadelphia to New Jersey was completed in 1954. The last leg, the 100-mile Northeast Extension, which went up to Scranton, opened in November 1957.

Walter A. Jones—Indefatigable Chairman

That the Pennsylvania Turnpike was completed by its deadline was due to the fact that one man was in the right place at the right time. Probably no other person at that time had the experience, drive, and dogged determination to get the job done possessed by Walter A. Jones.

George H. Earle won the 1934 election for governor. Among those who contributed to his campaign was Jones, a retired oil executive from Pittsburgh. To pay a political debt, Governor Earle appointed Jones chairman of the newly formed Pennsylvania Turnpike Commission in 1937. Among his first tasks was to buy the railbed of the old South Penn Railroad, over which the new highway would be built. He learned that the land was owned by two railroads, the Baltimore and Ohio and the Pennsylvania Railroad. The two companies asked a total of $9 million for the entire property. Jones thought the price was horrendously high, so he haggled them down to $1 million each. He was pleased with the deal—until he found out that his commission had no money to make the payments!

To finance the road, the commissioners issued $60 million in bonds in 1938. However, none of the New York bond houses would touch them because there was no precedent on which to judge their value. Undaunted, Jones approached President Franklin Delano Roosevelt. After hearing Jones' story, the president wrote an eight-word memorandum to Harold L.

Ickes of the Public Works Administration: "Give Walter Jones $20,000,000 for the Pennsylvania Turnpike." The amount was eventually increased to $26 million.

Investors were still unwilling to buy the bonds, so Jones returned to Washington and persuaded the Reconstruction Finance Corporation (RFC) to advance the rest of the money he needed. He was just in time; the WPA deadline for starting new projects had almost run out. The RFC okayed the money on October 8, 1938, and Jones got the word two days later. The deadline to start work was November 1.

Once the work started, Jones drove his contractors, and himself, so hard that his health broke down. He was hospitalized, but he never fully recovered. His poor health forced him to resign in 1942, and a year later, at the age of 68, he died.

Sea, Rail, and Air

THE FIRST STEAM-DRIVEN BOATS

By the late 18th century, steam-powered pumps and other machinery were being used for mining in Great Britain. Since the big money at the time was in commercial water transport, inventors were busy trying to use steam to propel boats. Most of these experiments were being done in the United States because great rivers like the Hudson and the Mississippi were ideally suited for steamboat travel.

During the 1780s, about a half-dozen steamboats of various types were being tested on rivers along the East Coast. Hardly anyone noticed, and the few people who watched these contraptions chug, sputter, and splash thought it was the funniest thing they ever saw. Five men built and successfully operated steamboats before 1790: Nathan Reade of Salem, Massachusetts; Samuel Morey of Fairlee, Vermont; John Fitch of Connecticut; James Rumsey of Shepherdstown, Virginia; and William Henry of Lancaster, Pennsylvania.

Fitch the Unlucky

Of this group, the best known was John Fitch, a brass founder and silversmith who conceived the idea of a steamboat in 1785. That same year, he completed his first model, a sidewheeler, and tested it on the Schuylkill River. Two years later, the delegates of the Constitutional Convention in Philadelphia took a break and went down to the docks on the Delaware to watch Fitch demonstrate his steamboat. It had 12 paddles, six on each side, attached to an overhead beam. A 12-inch cylinder engine lifted the paddles, moved them forward, dipped them in the water, and pulled the paddles rearward, thus propelling the boat forward. When moving, the boat looked like a huge spider walking on the water.

Over the next five years, Fitch continued to experiment and improve his boat, then received a patent for his invention. By 1790, he was running a ferry service between Philadelphia and Burlington, New Jersey, at the speed of eight miles an hour. Unfortunately, he never made a dime, and he went out of business. Nevertheless, Fitch operated the first steamboat business in America.

Fitch's life was a continuing run of bad luck. His father was a tyrant. He had a dishonest master during his apprenticeship. The woman he married turned out to be a violent bully. His idea for steam travel was 20 years ahead of its time, meaning nobody took him seriously, and he lived in a constant state of poverty.

Fitch made a trip to England to garner financial backers, but received only shrugs and scorn. His plans, models, and money gone, he worked as a common seaman aboard a ship in order to get passage back to America. In 1798, suffering from alcoholism, he died—some say of suicide—on the Kentucky frontier.

Robert Fulton

While John Fitch was unlucky most of his life, Robert Fulton spent his life converting adversity into his own good luck. Fulton did not invent the steamboat, but he made its use practical and profitable.

Fulton was born in 1765 on a farm near Quarryville in southern Lancaster County. From early on, he had an avid interest in art and mechanics. When a schoolmate threw away some paints and brushes, Fulton salvaged them—and that was the beginning of his art career. Before he was a teenager, he was making his own lead pencils and showed promise as an expert draftsman. At the age of 13 he invented a roman candle, which caused a sensation at Lancaster's Fourth of July celebration.

Young Fulton often visited William Henry, who had made some experiments with a steamboat. Using Henry's plans, he made a hand-cranked paddle wheel and attached it to a rowboat. However, at this point in his life, art was his main interest.

When Fulton was 17, his mother secured him an apprenticeship with a silversmith in Philadelphia, but it was not for him. He quit and set himself up as a painter of miniatures. Before the advent of photography, miniature portraits were a popular keepsake, often carried in lockets. Fulton garnered enough clients to support himself for four years in a small studio at Second and Walnut Streets in Philadelphia.

In 1787, a friend convinced Fulton to go to England and study art under the tutorship of a Chester County native, Benjamin West. As a successful artist, West was friendly with many of the kingdom's power-brokers, and he introduced Fulton to the Duke of Bridgewater, the founder of the British canal system, who induced the young American to abandon art and take up the study of mechanical science.

Fulton soon invented a double-inclined plane to raise or lower boats from one level to another. In 1794, he designed a mill for sawing marble; in 1796, he devised a cast iron aqueduct that was erected over the River Dee in the Grampian region of Scotland. Fulton designed several bridges; he also invented a machine for spinning flax, another for making ropes, one for digging ditches, and a dispatch boat.

In 1797, Fulton was living in Paris, where he built the *Nautilus*, a five-man submarine that could dive to depths of 25 feet and had a "torpedo" that could be attached to the hull of a ship and then detonated. Fulton demonstrated his submarine several times to a committee appointed by Napoleon Bonaparte. It dove to various depths and even stayed underwater for four hours. But the French turned down a chance to buy Fulton's submarine, and that put an end to underwater warfare for the next 60 years. The English were interested in his underwater craft, but Fulton refused to sell it because Great Britain and the United States were not on good terms at the time. (It was a good decision because both countries came to blows in the War of 1812.)

Fulton's Folly

While in France, Fulton met Robert R. Livingston, who became his patron. Livingston was the American ambassador to France who negotiated the Louisiana Purchase. A wealthy businessman, Livingston owned a 20-year monopoly on the development of steam transportation over the rivers and lakes of New York State. All he needed was someone with a steamboat.

On October 10, 1802, Fulton and Livingston signed a contract. Fulton agreed to design a steamboat that would travel up and down the Hudson River between New York City and Albany. Livingston, in turn, had the money to buy the material and the political clout to gain the proper permits and licenses. Marketing would be no problem. Sailing ships took four days to make the 145-mile trip from New York City to the state capital. If Fulton's steam-powered vessel could do it in half that time, the partners could build a fleet and make millions.

After a 19-year absence, Fulton returned to the United States in 1806 and set to work immediately on designing and building a boat. It was flat-bottomed, 146 feet long, and 12 feet wide. To propel it through the water, he mounted 15-foot-long paddle wheels on both sides, powered by a 24-horsepower Bolton and Watt engine from England. Fulton dubbed it the *Clermont*, which was the name of his partner's estate near Albany. Onlookers called it "Fulton's Folly."

On August 17, 1807, Fulton fired up his steamboat's coal furnace. The boiler pumped steam into the pistons; the paddle wheels began to churn up the water; gradually the boat inched out of its Greenwich Village berth and chugged upriver at four and a half miles per hour. The *Clermont* did not take the anticipated two days to reach Albany; it made the trip in just 32 hours.

In its first year, the *Clermont* took in $16,000. Fulton sank the profits into building more steam-powered boats, ferries, and other watercraft. Other entrepreneurs dove into the steamboat business and copied Fulton's plans. Consequently, Fulton and Robert Livingston spent a lot of time and money in court, suing people for infringing on their patent and protecting their monopoly.

In February 1815, Fulton and his legal team had just finished another legal battle in a Trenton, New Jersey, courtroom, and were returning by boat to New York City. As their boat entered New York's harbor, it hit some ice and Fulton's attorney fell overboard. The other men got soaked dragging him to safety. Fulton, now 49 years of age (considered old at the time), was worn out by all the legal battles. He came down with pneumonia and his doctor ordered him to stay in bed.

But Fulton, ignoring the pleas of his wife and his doctor's orders, left his sickbed and went to his shipyard at Paulus Hook, now Jersey City, to supervise the building of the *Fulton I*. This was not an ordinary job; the *Fulton I* was the world's first steam-powered battleship. For several days he stood for three hours at a time, sometimes in a cold rain, to watch, to advise, and to encourage his workmen. Days later, the pneumonia and physical stress got to him, and on February 24, 1815, he died.

FAREWELL FULTON

Robert Fulton, the man who revolutionized water transportation, lay in state in New York City and was buried at Trinity Church, after the biggest funeral that the city had ever seen. The state legislature declared six weeks of mourning. The grave of this famous Pennsylvanian can be found in Trinity Churchyard, just off Broadway at the head of Wall Street.

☞ *To Visit: Robert Fulton Birthplace*

A little stone house sits in the rolling hills of the Conowingo countryside. Robert Fulton lived here until he was two years old. It caught fire in 1822 and almost burned to the ground. Later it was rebuilt from the rubble and stands today, proud and refurbished, as a memorial to American inventiveness and to the genius who was born under its roof. The Robert Fulton Birthplace is now part of the Pennsylvania Trail of History, owned and operated by the Pennsylvania Historical and Museum Commission.

Robert Fulton Birthplace
RD 1
Quarryville, PA 17566
717-548-2679
Hours: Tuesday-Saturday, 8:30 A.M.-5 P.M.; Sunday, 1-5 P.M.

Robert Fulton was born in 1765 in this house, just off U.S. Route 222 below Quarryville in southern Lancaster County. This building had be restored after a fire in 1822 almost destroyed it.
Courtesy of the Pennsylvania Historical and Museum Commission

THE FIRST IRON STEAMBOAT

Before the days of canals and railroads, the merchants of Baltimore tried to get richer by hauling lumber, iron, and whiskey up and down the Susquehanna River. They spent a lot of money clearing the river of obstructions and removing rocky channels so that arks, boats, and rafts could navigate the river. They also constructed a canal from Port Deposit, Maryland, northward to Columbia, Pennsylvania. Parts of this canal can still be seen today alongside U.S. Route 222 in Maryland.

Next, they built the *Susquehanna*, a small steamboat, at Port Deposit. A posse of men pulled it nine miles up the Maryland Canal, but when it got stuck at the Conewago Falls, they gave up.

Then a businessman named Winchester had an idea. He got on his horse and rode to a place above the falls near the town of York Haven, Pennsylvania, where he contracted with an iron foundry to build another boat with a hull made out of sheet iron. When the hull was completed, it was placed on a huge wagon pulled by eight draft horses and hauled to Keesey's Ferry, now Wrightsville, on the Susquehanna. Christened the *Codurus*, it was launched on November 22, 1825, and fitted with an engine, machinery, and side paddle wheels. The *Codurus* was the first iron steamboat built in the United States and the first vessel of any kind fueled by anthracite.

On to New York

In April 1826, the *Codurus* headed upstream to Binghamton, New York, with its designer, Captain John Elgar, at the helm. The sight of Elgar's steam-belching boat created quite a stir at every town and hamlet along the river; he was greeted with a grand reception at every port of call. Eventually, the *Codurus* reached Binghamton, and then started back. The 300-mile round trip took three slow, arduous months. The *Codurus* has the distinction of being the only steamboat ever to navigate the Susquehanna from York County to Binghamton.

The boat returned to York Haven on July 17, 1826. Captain Elgar flatly stated, "Steam navigation on the Susquehanna is impractical," so its owners in Baltimore moved the history-making boat to North Carolina, where it spent its final years hauling freight and passengers on the inland waterways.

ALL ABOARD!

The first railroad in Pennsylvania, and the first in America to be surveyed, was built by Thomas Leiper. His crew started to work on it in 1809 and finished it in 1810. The rails were strips of oak plank over which a horse could pull three times its own weight quite easily. There was probably only one car, which was simply a huge box similar to a mine car mounted on cast-iron wheels. The driver sat on the front end of the horse-drawn car. Leiper's line ran less than a mile and carried stone from his quarry on Crum Creek to the landing on Ridley Creek in Delaware County.

The Stourbridge Lion

The Delaware and Hudson Canal Company in northeastern Pennsylvania decided to replace the mules that pulled coal cars from the mines to the canal with steam locomotives, which had been invented in England by George Stephenson in 1825. In 1828, the company sent one of its engineers, Horatio Allen, to England to buy one of these new steam engines. He purchased one called the "Lion" from a locomotive works in Stourbridge, plus two others from the Stephenson works in Newcastle. The locomotives were brought in one piece to the United States on a ship.

On August 8, 1829, the "Stourbridge Lion" became the first locomotive to run on a railroad track in the United States. The Lion was too heavy for the wooden rails and was replaced by a lighter lokie, the "America." The Lion was taken apart. Its boiler was used in the company's shop while the rest was put under a shed to rust in peace. In 1889, what was left of the Stourbridge Lion was sent to the Smithsonian Institution. Today, an exact replica of the Lion is on display in a special building in Honesdale, Wayne County.

The "Stourbridge Lion," a steam locomotive, was purchased in England by Horatio Alger in 1828. A huge lion's head was emblazoned on the front of the boiler. The Delaware and Hudson Canal Company planned to use the locomotive on their line between Carbondale, Lackawanna County, and Honesdale, Wayne County, but it proved too heavy for American tracks. This is an illustration of the locomotive's trial run. *Courtesy of the Wayne County Historical Society, Honesdale, PA*

☞ To Visit: Wayne County Historical Society

The society runs a museum and a reference library that is excellent for genealogical searches.

Wayne County Historical Society
804 Main Street
Honesdale, PA 18431
717-253-3240
Museum e-mail: wchs@ptd.net
Library e-mail: wchpa@ptd.net
Hours: Wednesday-Saturday, 10 A.M.-4 P.M.
Admission charged.

THE IRON HORSE

Many important developments in railroading took place in Pennsylvania. Ironically, some of the steam pioneers were not engineers, but watchmakers. In 1831, the Baltimore and Ohio Railroad (B&O) held a contest to find their own American-made, coal-burning locomotive. Of those who competed, three were watchmakers, including Stacy Costell and Zeke Childs of Philadelphia.

The winner of the $4,000 prize was Phineas Davis, a watchmaker whose shop was located at the corner of King and Newberry Streets in York. He built the first coal-burning locomotive in America and named it, after his hometown, the "York." It pulled a train of five cars, carrying 150 passengers at 15 miles per hour between Baltimore and Ellicott Mills, Maryland.

In 1833, Davis built a much larger passenger hauler, the "Atlantic," a seven-ton brute that stayed in operation for 60 years. The piston rods were connected with the cranks by overhead rocking beams attached to the boiler, from which long connecting rods passed down to the cranks, resembling the hind legs of a grasshopper—hence its name, the "grasshopper engine." Also, it was the first locomotive that had coupled wheels and a double instead of a single pair of drive wheels. On September 27, 1835, Davis died in, of all things, a wreck of one of the trains he had built.

In 1835, William Norris of Philadelphia built the "George Washington," the first locomotive that could pull a load of over eight tons up a 7 percent incline without the help of railroad hoists. It ran on the Columbia and Philadelphia Line, the forerunner of the Pennsylvania Railroad.

CLANG! CLANG! GOES THE TROLLEY

Charles Van Depoele, from Belgium, began experimenting with electric cars in 1882, at the age of 36. On November 26, 1886, he tested America's first electrically powered street car on the Scranton Suburban Railway. It attained a speed of 12 miles per hour and ran 100 miles daily. The little wheels that rolled on the overhead wires fed 1,400 volts to the car's motor and were called travellers. Leo Daft, another streetcar inventor, called them trollers—hence the name trolley cars.

THE FIRST FLIGHT?

According to the records of the "Old Wenrich Church of Dauphin County," the first airplane built and demonstrated in the United States was the work of the Pennsylvania Dutch brothers George and Christian Peltz of Linglestown, a suburb of Harrisburg. George was less than 20 years old when he and his brother worked in a shed throughout the autumn of 1828, building an "airship." Their invention was described as a boxlike structure with wings on both sides. Mounted on each wing was a series of paddles. Seated inside, the operators turned a hand crank to induce a flapping or revolving motion of the paddles.

When the plane was completed, George invited his family and neighbors to witness the initial flight. The brothers planned to fly north across the Blue Mountain to the home of their grandparents, who resided in Piketown. The brothers hoisted the plane to the top of a tree, stepped inside, and began to crank furiously. George shouted, "Now I go for my dinner at Piketown." The aircraft, with all the swiftness and grace of a rock, plunged to the ground. The bulk of the aircraft fell on top of George, crushing him to death. His brother Christian escaped with a broken arm.

Today, the graves of George and Christian Peltz are in the cemetery next to St. Thomas United Church of Christ (long known as Wenrich's Church), located on Pennsylvania Route 39, about one mile east of Linglestown.

ANOTHER FIRST FLIGHT

Gustav Whitehead immigrated to the United States from Germany in 1895. For the next three years, he moved wherever he could find work. He made gliders in Boston and buggies in Buffalo. In 1897, he came to Pennsylvania and briefly stayed in Johnstown before moving to Bates Street in Pittsburgh. He worked in a coal mine and did odd jobs. During his spare time, Whitehead set up a workshop where he started to build a flying machine with the assistance of his friend Louis Darvarich. To power his aircraft, Whitehead experimented with steam engines and lightweight boilers, testing them late into the night until they burst. With all the noise and safety hazards he created, no wonder Whitehead became the most hated man on Bates Street.

The boilers provided steam for a piston engine that turned a propeller in a motion similar to the drive wheels on a locomotive. A propeller was attached to each wing. The German inventor tested his contraption in Pittsburgh's Schenley Park in April or May of 1898—more than five years before the Wright brothers' famous first flight. Darvarich stoked the engine's boiler while Whitehead, perched in front, steered. The aircraft flew a half mile at an altitude of 20 or 30 feet. The flight came to an abrupt halt when the aircraft rammed a building. Whitehead was not injured but the hot steam scalded Darvarich.

There is no evidence to support this incident: no photos of the aircraft, no news stories, and no record of treatment for the alleged injuries in the police, fire department, or hospital files in Pittsburgh.

Whitehead and Darvarich left Pittsburgh on bicycles in 1900 and wound up as coal truck drivers in Bridgeport, Connecticut. Whitehead continued to build airplanes until 1908. He died on October 10, 1927.

(By the way...what keeps this story alive, especially among some Connecticut scholars, are affidavits filed between 1934 and 1936 by some witnesses, including a sworn statement by Louis Darvarich.)

AIRPORT FIRSTS

Western Pennsylvania's first major airport, Bettis Airport, was built in West Mifflin, southeast of Pittsburgh, and was operable by 1925. Two years later, it was being used on a regular basis by the U.S. Airmail Service. Mail destined for airplane delivery took to the air by unusual means in those days: A long cable was tightly strung between two high poles. A large canvas mail bag was hung by a heavy wire on the cable midway between the two posts. An aircraft swooped down and flew about 30 feet above the ground with a hooklike arm extended from its fuselage. When the hook made contact with the cable, it quickly grabbed the mailbag and pulled it into the aircraft. This enabled the plane to pick up the mail without having to land!

The Allegheny County Airport opened in 1931 and had the first hard-surfaced runway in the country. It was also the third largest airport in the United States at the time. It drew so much business away from Bettis that the old field was relegated to a pilot training facility.

Bettis Field and its surrounding area were purchased in 1948 by the Westinghouse Corporation for its Atomic Power Division. It was here that the power plant for the first nuclear-powered submarine, the USS *Nautilus*, launched in 1954, was built.

THE FIRST INTERNATIONAL FLIGHT

Born in Brookville, Jefferson County, Earl Sandt moved to Erie, where he eventually opened the Star Garage. He tinkered with everything from airplanes to automobiles. In 1911, he purchased a secondhand Curtis biplane. He borrowed two Indian motorcycle gas tanks from LeJeal's store on Sassafras Street and attached them to his aircraft. On February 20, 1912, Sandt filled these tanks with gasoline and took off into history by making the first flight across Lake Erie.

Thirty-five minutes later, he landed on a patch of ice near the lighthouse at Long Pont, Canada, to become the first pilot to make an international flight in a motor-powered aircraft. The astonished lighthouse keeper gave him a cup of coffee and sold him gasoline from his motorboat so Sandt could fly back to Pennsylvania.

But he didn't make it. Sandt ran out of fuel and crash-landed his plane at 90 miles per hour on the ice-covered Lake Erie. He was not injured, but he had to walk five miles across the ice. He reached Harborcreek in time to catch the last evening trolley to Erie.

Sandt became an instant worldwide celebrity. But he was only to enjoy his celebrity status for a short two years. In 1914, while putting on an exhibition at the Grove City College commencement, he hit a garage on take-off and broke his leg. Gangrene set in. Within 10 days he was dead.

THE PARACHUTE

Stephan Banic was born on November 23, 1870, at Smolenice in the Trnava region of Slovakia when it was part of the Austro-Hungarian empire. He immigrated to the United States in 1907 and worked in the bituminous mines near Greenville, Mercer County. During his spare time he invented the first parachute, for which he obtained U.S. patent number 1,108,484 in 1914. He donated his patent to the United States Army Air Corps for a token fee: an honorary membership in the corps.

After World War I, in 1921, the Slovak inventor returned to his native Slovakia and worked as a stone mason. As a hobby, Banic explored underground caverns and was the co-discoverer of the Drina Cave in eastern Europe.

Banic died in 1941. A memorial tablet hailing him as the inventor of the parachute was unveiled at the Bratislava Airport in Slovakia in 1970. His grave marker in a Smolenice cemetery is an inverted cone-shaped piece of marble, resembling an open parachute with a bas-relief of a paratrooper.

THE FORERUNNER OF THE HELICOPTER

The autogiro is a regular airplane with three or four very long propeller blades mounted on a structure built over the fuselage, similar to a helicopter. But unlike a helicopter, which has blades driven by an engine, an autogiro has no motor to drive its big blades. Instead, the motor-driven propeller on the front of the aircraft produces a backwash of wind that

The Pitcairn PCA-2 Autogiro landing on the White House lawn in 1931.
Courtesy of Steven Pitcairn, Pitcairn Aviation, Bryn Athyn, PA

turns the big blades on top, giving the plane extra "lift." Some autogiros have stubby wings; some have no wings; but all autogiros have horizontal and vertical stabilizers in the back of the fuselage to steer and control the aircraft.

The speed of an autogiro ranges from 30 to 120 miles per hour. It cannot hover in the air like a helicopter, but it can take off in a small space and land almost straight down. To demonstrate this capability, the Pitcairn-Cierva Company of Willow Grove, Montgomery County, did a publicity stunt on April 22, 1931. One of the company's pilots, James Garrett Ray of Philadelphia, landed an autogiro on the White House lawn (with permission, of course). He was the first to do so and was awarded the 1930 Collier Trophy by President Herbert Hoover.

Cierva and Pitcairn Join Forces

Juan de la Cierva constructed the first successful autogiro; it was flown from his native Spain in 1923. Five years later, Cierva flew an autogiro across the English Channel. A businessman in Willow Grove named Harold Frederick Pitcairn heard about Cierva's invention and arranged passage to the United States for the Spaniard and his autogiro.

Pitcairn started flying as a teenager and, at age 26, opened a landing strip near his family's glass factory at Bryn Athyn, Montgomery County, in 1923. His business grew so quickly that, in 1925, he purchased a sprawling chunk of level ground at nearby Willow Grove. He started to take people on chartered air trips, conduct flying lessons, and give short rides for a small fee. By October 1927, Pitcairn Aviation had carried over 30,000 passengers, mostly on short hops. In 1927, the U.S. government awarded Pitcairn a contract to fly an overnight mail route between New York City and Atlanta, Georgia. Two years later, he sold his mail and passenger routes plus his flying school to the North American Company, which became Eastern Airlines. Pitcairn used the profits from this sale to start manufacturing a very unusual aircraft.

Two autogiros, the PCA-1B and the PCA-2, flying over the docks of New York City in 1930.
Courtesy of Steven Pitcairn, Pitcairn Aviation, Bryn Athyn, PA

Juan de la Cierva arrived in Bryn Athyn on December 17, 1928. Two days later, Pitcairn flew the first autogiro in this country, the C8 Mark II, which was remodeled from an English biplane. The two men organized the Pitcairn-Cierva Autogiro Company for licensing the manufacture of the autogiro in the United States.

Autogiro Firsts

To promote his autogiro, Pitcairn made several "firsts," including:
- The first intercity autogiro flight—Pitcairn took off from Philadelphia on May 13, 1929, and flew to Langley Field, Virginia, where he exhibited and tested his Cierva autogiro at the fourth annual meeting of the National Advisory Committee for Aeronautics.
- The first transcontinental autogiro flight—Pitcairn's employee, John MacDonald Miller, left Willow Grove in "The Missing Link" (PCA-2)

on May 14, 1931. Stopping frequently to exhibit the machine, he landed at the North Island Naval Air Station, San Diego, California, on May
14, 1931.

- Pitcairn made the first sale of an autogiro in 1931 to the *Detroit News*.
The newspaper purchased a Pitcairn PCA-2, which was flown on
February 12, 1931, from Willow Grove to the Motor City to be used for
publicity purposes, as were many autogiros. Sponsors painted their
sales messages on the sides of the fuselage. Beech Nut chewing gum
had the most famous autogiro pilot—Amelia Earhart, who referred to
the plane as a "flying billboard." Miss Earhart was the first woman pilot
of an autogiro as well as the first pilot to carry a passenger; it happened
on December 19, 1930, at Pitcairn Field in Willow Grove. She also set an
altitude record of 18,415 feet—over three miles high—at Willow Grove
in 1931. She then flew her Pitcairn "Beech Nut Special" to a cross-country record, but crashed in Texas. Luckily, she was not injured.

THE FIRST COMMUTER'S DREAM MACHINE

Harold F. Pitcairn tried to replace the automobile with the autogiro in 1936.
He built a single-seater and used it to commute between his home in Bryn
Athyn and his factory in Willow Grove. Upon landing, he shut off the propeller, then folded up the wings and rotary blades. He reboarded the autogiro, shifted gears on the engine to operate the rear wheel, then drove from
a landing strip at about five miles per hour to his house. With the country
mired in the Great Depression, hardly anybody could afford to pay $12,000
for this autogiro. The project never got off the ground.

In 1941, the U.S. Navy purchased Pitcairn's airfield and renamed it the
U.S. Naval Air Station at Willow Grove.

Eat and Drink Up

BUBBLE GUM

Walter E. Diemer invented the world's first commercial bubble gum in 1928 when he was working for the Fleer Corporation in Philadelphia. "It was an accident. I was doing something else and ended up with something with bubbles," said Diemer in an interview in 1966. "The purpose of the experiments was to come up with a chewing gum base that we had been buying from another company."

Fleer sold a test batch in a Philadelphia grocery store. The sample sold out in one afternoon. Diemer then taught Fleer salesmen how to blow bubbles, so they could demonstrate the product when they traveled from store to store selling the penny-a-piece gum. Afterwards, bubble gum—which traditionally gets its flavor from a mix of wintergreen, peppermint, vanilla, and cinnamon—quickly spread around the world.

Almost three-quarters of a century later, Diemer still could not believe "all the bubble gum in the world came from my five-pound batch. It's the most popular confection in the world." Like the first batch he produced, it is also colored pink. "It's the only color I had and it's been the standard ever since."

Diemer was born in Philadelphia in 1904 and worked for the Fleer Corporation until he retired as senior vice president in 1970, then continued on as a member of the board of directors for 10 years. He moved to Lancashire Terrace Retirement Village in Lancaster. On January 9, 1998, at the age of 93, Walter E. Diemer died of congestive heart failure.

STORY WITH A TWIST

In the 1850s, a tramp was walking through Lititz in Lancaster County. He stopped at Ambrose Rauch's bake shop to beg for food. Rauch graciously gave the traveler a meal. In return the tramp gave Rauch his "secret recipe" for hard pretzels. Rauch tossed it aside. Julius Sturgis, an apprentice of Rauch's, picked up the recipe and kept it. A few years later, in 1861, Sturgis opened his own bake shop, which exclusively produced the unique snack. Thus was created the first commercial pretzel bakery in the Western Hemisphere.

Of course, most pretzels are topped with salt, which brings up the story of that condiment.

SALT

Before the invention of ice boxes and refrigerators, food was preserved by salting. Salt was so important in ancient times that it was often used for money. The word *salary* is derived from the Latin word *salarium*, meaning the salt that was given to Roman soldiers as part of their pay.

Tradition credits a Mrs. Deemer of Indiana County with the discovery of salt in Pennsylvania when, in 1810, she found the food she cooked in water that trickled from rocks near the Conemaugh River had a salty taste.

A profitable salt industry grew up after Bill Johnson drilled the first salt well in 1813 near the present-day town of Saltsburg. By 1840, there were 21 salt works and 24 wells along the Conemaugh as the industry was spreading throughout western Pennsylvania. A nuisance that these old salt drillers encountered was oil mixed in with the salt brine. Some salt wells turned out to be actual oil gushers!

Since these were the days before anybody had any use for oil, the well owners simply spilled the oil on the ground or ran it into the Pennsylvania Canal. This angered the canal boat owners because the gooey slick ruined their hemp cables and messed up the new paint on their boats.

ICE CREAM

Headquartered in Pittsburgh, Sam Isaly ran a string of confection shops that stretched from Uniontown to Erie. One of the most popular and unusual offerings in his stores was the "skyscraper" cone. Instead of using the standard spherical scoop, Isaly devised a special long, triangular scoop that produced a six- to eight-inch-tall, narrow, triangular chunk of ice cream that sat on top of a cone. Hence the name skyscraper.

It took much training and practice by a strong-armed soda jerk to scoop a good skyscraper cone. As prices of ice cream skyrocketed in the 1970s, the skyscraper cone was discontinued.

Isaly did invent something else that has become a national favorite. In 1929, he dipped a vanilla ice cream bar in chocolate, packaged it in a silver foil wrapper, and called it the Klondike Bar.

Frank Blandi owned the LeMont Restaurant at the Park Schenley hotel, where he created a treat that has become a staple in restaurants around the country—a scoop of vanilla ice cream rolled in a creamy pecan sauce—the pecan roll.

This is part of a promotional poster that hung in "Sweet Shops" throughout western Pennsylvania advertising Isaly's "skyscraper" cone of ice cream, the first of its kind in the country. *Courtesy of Jay Dery, Evans City, PA*

THE FIRST CANDY COMPANY TOWN

There are plenty of towns, villages, and patches in this country that were owned and built by coal, rail, and iron companies to house their employees. But nowhere in the country except Pennsylvania is there a town that owes its existence to candy.

After several attempts—and failures—to make candy in Philadelphia, New York, and Colorado, Milton Snavely Hershey, from Lancaster County, finally found success making chocolate candy in Dauphin County. In 1903, Hershey bought a cornfield in Derry Township and cre-

This is the corner of Chocolate and Cocoa Avenues in Hershey, Pennsylvania, the first candy company town in the United States. Note the street lamps in the shape of Hershey's Kisses.

ated a chocolate manufacturing center, now known as the Hershey Foods Corporation. He then went on to build a town for his employees, named (you guessed it) Hershey. Hershey had no children of his own, but to give his workers and their families a place to enjoy themselves when not at work, he built an amusement park, now called Hersheypark.

WATCH WHAT YOU EAT!

Sarah Tyson Rorer was born in Richboro, Bucks County, in 1849. Her life-long work in nutrition earned her the distinction of being the country's first dietitian. She first taught cooking at Philadelphia's New Century Club in 1881. Three years later, she opened that city's School of Cooking and Diet. She emphasized that all disease, except contagious types, could be avoided by following a proper diet.

Rorer then developed a lecture series for students at the Philadelphia Women's Medical College whose focus was chemistry and the nutritive value of food as it relates to health and disease. At the urging of several well-known physicians in that city, she founded a dietary kitchen where prescriptions for foods to treat special diseases could be filled in a scientific manner. This led to her establishment of the first dietary counseling service in the country.

Rorer went into the publishing business in 1886 with her famous *Philadelphia Cook Book* and a monthly magazine on cooking and household arts called *Table Talk*. Over a period of 35 years, she wrote over 50 cookbooks. For years she was in demand as a lecturer on the therapeutics of diet across the United States and at World's Fairs.

In her later years, Rorer went broke through bad investments. Refusing any aid except for donations from friends, she lived with her son on a small farm in Colebrook, Lebanon County. She went blind in 1937, but until her death at the age of 88, she helped prepare food for sick and impoverished infants.

POP GOES THE WATER

The man who first made carbonated water spent his later years in Northumberland County, Pennsylvania, and it all started when he discovered oxygen.

Nobody knew anything about oxygen until 1774, when it was discovered by a minister whose hobbies were chemistry and rabble-rousing. His name? Joseph Priestley. He found that when he heated red oxide of mercury, a gas escaped, which he called "dephlogisticated air." (Twenty years later a French scientist, Antoine Lavoisier, named this gas oxygen.)

On filling an inverted beer glass with oxygen, Priestley noticed that when he placed a lit candle inside, it burned brighter, and when a mouse breathed the gas in the glass, the animal became more active.

During the mid-1700s, it was believed that sea scurvy was caused by a lack of "fixed air" in the human body. Priestley tried to produce "fixed air" by mixing chalk with sulfuric acid and injecting it in water. The result was carbonated water, an essential ingredient in many of today's soft drinks. Priestley's "soft drink" tasted awful and could not be marketed. Nevertheless, the Royal Society was so impressed that it awarded him the Copley Medal, its highest honor in chemistry.

FIRST SODA POP

By the way...in 1807, Townsend Speakman, a druggist in Philadelphia, took Joseph Priestley's carbonated water, mixed fruit flavors with it, and turned out the world's first soda pop, which he called Nephite Julep.

Priestley was born in Fieldhead, England, in 1733, the son of a woolen cloth dresser. His parents died when he was a child, and he was raised by an aunt in an environment of free religious discussion. Because of his aunt's influence, he studied for the ministry and became a teacher of history and science. In his spare time, he conducted scientific experiments until 1773, when Lord Shelburne became his benefactor and Priestley could devote full time to his own projects.

Priestley Comes to America

While working on his experiments, Priestley made the acquaintance of Benjamin Franklin, then living in London. Priestley supported the rights of the American colonists, but he got into trouble in the early 1790s when he sided with the French revolutionists and thereby incurred the wrath of the British public. Priestley's book, *The Corruption of Christianity*, made him the most hated man in England. In 1791, a mob broke into his home and destroyed everything, including his laboratory equipment, a 30,000-volume library, and his diaries. Although the British government reimbursed him for the damage, Priestley and his wife left England and arrived in Philadelphia in August 1794.

After finding the cost of living too expensive in the City of Brotherly Love, the Priestleys moved to the town of Northumberland, where Dr. Thomas Cooper was planning to establish a colony of English refugees. There, Priestley built a two-story house with a large yard that extended to the banks of the north branch of the Susquehanna River. Priestley lived out his remaining years in Northumberland, making occasional trips to Philadelphia to preach or to address the American Philosophical Society.

After his death in 1804, the Priestley house passed through the hands of several owners. In 1919, a professor at Pennsylvania State University bought it, planning to move the structure to the campus, many miles away in State College. This idea was later abandoned and the university operated the building as a museum until it was given to the town of Northumberland in 1955. In 1960, the Pennsylvania Historical and Museum Commission took over the administration of the house.

☞ *To Visit: The Joseph Priestley House*

Today the Priestley house stands much as it did when the famous pioneer chemist lived there in 1800. It contains a small museum with Priestley's personal effects.

The Joseph Priestley House
472 Priestley Avenue
Northumberland, PA 17857
717-473-9474
Hours: Tuesday-Saturday, 8:30 A.M.-5 P.M.; Sunday, 1-5 P.M.
In winter months, Tuesday-Saturday, 9 A.M.-4:30 P.M.;
Sunday, 1-4:30 P.M.
Admission charged.

Joseph Priestley, the man who first made carbonated water, spent the last years of his life in this house in Northumberland. *Courtesy of the Pennsylvania Historical and Museum Commission*

ICE CREAM SODA AND SUNDAES

Ice cream soda was invented in Philadelphia in 1874 when a soda jerk named Robert Green dropped a scoop of ice cream into a glass of soda. Ice cream sodas soon caught on and became popular across the country. Many ministers considered the concoction to be too sinfully enjoyable and frivolous to be consumed on a Sunday. Bowing to pressure from the clergy, many towns banned the tasty treat on the Sabbath. However, a few pharmacists in the early 1900s got around the ban by replacing the carbonated water and just serving ice cream topped with syrup, fruit, and candies. The new treat was first called a "Sunday" and, later, a sundae.

Time to Celebrate

Several red-letter days originated in Pennsylvania.

THE SHADOW KNO-O-OWS...

Although it is not a national holiday, Groundhog Day, February 2, is nationally recognized as the great day of weather prognostication when all eyes and ears turn to the borough of Punxsutawney, Jefferson County, to await the appearance of Punxsutawney Phil. If the Great Climatic Fortune-Teller emerges from his hole in the ground and sees his shadow, there will be six more weeks of winter; if he does not, spring is just around the corner. The Punxy Groundhog Club started this mock pagan ritual of weather forecasting atop Gobbler's Knob in 1884; its members dress up in tuxedos to mark the occasion.

The tradition of placing one's trust in an animal to forecast the weather goes back to the ancient Greeks, who believed that an animal's shadow was its soul, blackened by the past year's sins. During winter hibernation, the animal's soul is cleansed, but should the varmint awaken before winter is over, he will see his shadow and be horrified, returning to his den to give nature more time to purify his soul.

The Palatine Germans, ancestors of the Pennsylvania Dutch, associated this belief with the dachs, a badgerlike animal. When these Germans settled in Pennsylvania in the 18th century, they could not find a dachs, so they substituted the groundhog.

GRUNDSOWDAG

Groundhog Day could be considered the national holiday of the Pennsylvania Dutch because it is marked by many grand celebrations—from Grundsow Lodge Number Ains on Da Lechaw near Allentown, Lehigh County, to 15 others dotting the eastern part of the state from Stroudsburg, Monroe County, to Philadelphia. Probably the zaniest observance is held by the Slumbering Groundhog Lodge on the banks of Puddleduck Creek, just south of Quarryville, Lancaster County. Grown men, including prominent businessmen and politicians, cavort around in long white nightshirts and top hats. The initiates (new members) wear old-fashioned baby bonnets with pacifiers dangling from rope necklaces. It is the job of the "baby groundhogs" to cook and serve an elaborate breakfast on February 2 to the members and guests of the Slumbering Groundhog Lodge.

MEMORIAL DAY: A DAY FOR REMEMBRANCE

On July 4, 1864, Mrs. Sophie Keller Hall was on her way to the Lutheran cemetery at Boalsburg, Centre County, to place flowers on a soldier's grave. She met Miss Emma Hunter, who was going to the same churchyard to decorate the grave of her father, who had served as a surgeon in the Union Army. At the time, the Civil War was raging, so the ladies decided to put flowers on the graves of every soldier in the cemetery.

Their simple homage of decorating the graves of soldiers soon spread to other communities. Four years later, the idea reached General John Alexander Logan, commander in chief of the Grand Army of the Republic (the GAR was composed of Union veterans of the Civil War). On March 5, 1868, he issued General Order No. 11, which began, "The 30th day of May, 1868, is designated for the purpose of strewing with flowers, or otherwise decorating the graves of comrades who died in defense of their country during the late rebellion...."

For decades, May 30 was known as Decoration Day in the North and observed on a state-by-state basis. Later the day became known as Memorial Day. Finally, in 1971, the federal government made it an official national holiday.

MOM'S SPECIAL DAY

On May 8, 1914, President Woodrow Wilson approved a joint resolution of Congress that designated the second Sunday in May as Mother's Day. Anna Jarvis of Philadelphia was delighted. She'd led an 11-year campaign to establish a holiday to honor the memory of her mother and to celebrate all mothers, and now her wish had come true.

To the end, Jarvis devoted all her time to writing letters, traveling, and making speeches. The second Sunday in May was chosen for Mother's Day because on that day in 1905, Jarvis' mother, Anna Reeves Jarvis, died in Philadelphia. The custom of wearing carnations on this day goes back to when Anna was a child and her mother's flower garden was filled with carnations.

Born in 1864 in Grafton, West Virginia, Anna Jarvis moved to North 12th Street in Philadelphia in 1883 with her mother and her blind younger sister. Anna worked in an advertising agency until she was 41 years old. She decided to quit her job after her mother died and left her a large inheritance so that she could devote all her energies to establishing Mother's Day. She campaigned for the holiday in 43 countries, and she received so much mail in support of her efforts that she bought the house next door just to hold it all!

TOO MUCH OF A GOOD THING?

As the popularity of Mother's Day caught on around the country, Anna Jarvis grew more and more disillusioned. The holiday was becoming little more than another business opportunity for florists, candy makers, confectioners, and greeting card companies. Frustrated and angry, she wrote to hundreds of newspapers, "They're commercializing Mother's Day. I intended it to be a day of sentiment, not of profit." She raised so much ruckus that she was once sent to jail for disturbing the peace.

Anna died in 1948 at Marshall Square Sanitarium in West Chester, Chester County, bitter and sorry that she had ever started Mother's Day. (By the way, Miss Jarvis never married and was never herself a mother.)

FLAG DAY

June 14—Flag Day—was started by a man from Allentown, Lehigh County. In 1912, Joseph Hart persuaded the Benevolent and Protective Order of Elks, meeting in Atlantic City, that a "flag day" should be written in their bylaws and observed each June 14. Five years later, Hart urged President Woodrow Wilson to deliver a "flag day" address to the American people to honor the day that Congress adopted the stars and stripes as our national flag—June 14, 1777.

Pennsylvania became the first state to declare Flag Day a legal holiday on May 7, 1937 (Act No. 155). It designated June 14 as Flag Day and stipulated that the holiday be celebrated on Monday when it falls on Sunday. In 1949, President Harry Truman signed the bill that officially designated June 14 as Flag Day throughout the United States.

GIVING THANKS

Think of Thanksgiving Day and what pops into your head? Pilgrims and Indians feasting together in Massachusetts way back in the 1620s, right? Just exactly what they ate and whether they were breaking bread (or whatever) together back then is debatable. But what's certain is that the holiday as we now know it didn't become popular until almost two and a half centuries later.

The first official Thanksgiving Day in Pennsylvania was in 1817, when Governor Simon Snyder of Selinsgrove, Snyder County, designated the third Tuesday of November as the state's Thanksgiving holiday. The following year, Governor William Findlay of Mercersburg, Franklin County, set aside November 19 as Thanksgiving Day. But both declarations got little response from the citizens of the state. Some Pennsylvania Dutchmen resented the holiday because it conflicted with their Harvest Home Festival. Others simply ignored the holiday altogether. The governors got the message; no more proclamations about officially giving thanks were issued for two decades.

Governor David Rittenhouse Porter of Huntingdon County proclaimed December 21, 1843, as Thanksgiving Day that year, but there was no such observance in 1844. Finally, Governor Francis Shunk of Montgomery County designated November 27, 1845, as Thanksgiving Day. And Pennsylvanians have observed the holiday ever since.

But it was through the efforts of a Pennsylvania woman that Thanksgiving Day became a national holiday.

Going National

Governor Porter's Thanksgiving proclamation gave Sarah Josepha Buell Hale the idea that the holiday should be a national one and she decided to make it so. She was editor of *Godey's Lady's Book*, the most popular magazine in the country, published in Philadelphia, and she was in a good position to influence a lot of people. Being from New Hampshire, Hale promoted the New England version of the holiday, with Pilgrims and Indians and all. Each year the November issue of *Godey's Lady's Book* had stories of family reunions plus advice on how to stuff a turkey and make a mince pie. In addition to her editorials, Hale wrote letters to the governors of every state and territory, urging them to proclaim the last Thursday in November as Thanksgiving Day.

Other magazines joined her campaign with their articles on ways to celebrate Thanksgiving Day. A growing number of states declared it a holiday, but not Virginia; it was dead-set against the "Yankee Holiday" because the abolitionist preachers and politicians used the occasion to condemn slavery.

The Civil War put an end to slavery and made Hale's dream a reality. On October 3, 1863, President Lincoln responded to personal letters from Hale by proclaiming the last Thursday in November as a National Day of Thanksgiving.

SARAH HALE'S REAL CLAIM TO FAME

Despite her success as an editor and in getting Thanksgiving Day declared a national holiday, Sarah Hale is most famous to this day for her nursery rhyme, "Mary Had a Little Lamb."

CHRISTMAS TRADITIONS

Most of America's Christmas customs were first introduced by European immigrants living in Pennsylvania.

Trimming the Tree

Christmas trees started to appear in the Middle Ages when the Germans held an Adam and Eve religious holiday on September 24. Festivities included morality plays about life in the Garden of Eden, featuring evergreen trees decorated with apples to symbolize the fall of man. Afterwards, the peasants dragged the trees home to cut up for firewood. One Christmas someone decided to place candles on the tree to honor Christ as the Light of the World. The idea sparked a tradition.

A few centuries later, the American colonies were fighting for their independence from Great Britain. The British hired mercenaries from the German state of Hesse. Some of these Hessians were captured at the Battle of Trenton and brought to a prison at the Carlisle Barracks in Cumberland County. Some historians believe that in 1778, these Hessian prisoners at Carlisle put up the first Christmas tree in America. The first documented evidence of Christmas trees in the United States was cited by Matthew Zahn of Lancaster in his diary. The date: December 22, 1822.

Decorated Christmas trees in the home did not become popular in this country until after the Civil War. At first people made their own ornaments for the tree, but entrepreneurs soon realized there was money to be made in this new custom. In 1875, William Martin of Philadelphia patented a folded paper star to top off the tree. Seeing the popularity of imported German tinsel, Bernard Wilmsen, a Prussian immigrant, started a factory in the 1880s in Philadelphia to manufacture the first tinsel garlands and tinsel rope in the country.

Saving for Christmas

The first Christmas Club in the United States was started by the Carlisle Trust Company of Carlisle, Cumberland County, in 1909. Merkel Landis, the bank's treasurer, came up with the idea. The first payment was mailed on December 1, 1909.

Everyday Things

ROLL OUT THE PAPER

A businessman named Joseph C. Gayetty made the first commercially packaged toilet paper in 1857. The product was "unbleached pearl-colored pure manila hemp paper" with Gayetty's name watermarked on each sheet. He sold it as "Gayetty's Medicated Paper—a perfectly pure article for the toilet and for the prevention of piles." Sales stank because it was sold in packs of 500 single sheets for 50 cents a pack, which made it a pricey item in those days.

Then, in 1879, two brothers, Clarence and Edward Scott, started a paper products business in Philadelphia, just when many homeowners were installing indoor plumbing. The outhouse was moving in-house, and the Scotts saw a golden opportunity. They made the first bathroom tissue on small rolls that were sold in plain brown wrappers at rock-bottom prices. The Scott Paper Company was off and running.

THE ZIPPO LIGHTER

Used for starting campfires on windy days, or for lighting cigarettes on the deck of a ship at sea, the Zippo lighter is guaranteed to fire with every flick of the thumb, or it will be repaired free of charge by the manufacturer in the northwestern Pennsylvania town of Bradford, McKean County. This peerless lighter was invented during the Great Depression of the 1930s by George Grant Blaisdell.

The inventor of the Zippo lighter, George G. Blaisdell, pictured here holding a (large!) replica of a Zippo, circa 1940. *Courtesy of Zippo Manufacturing Co., Bradford, PA*

As a young man, Blaisdell earned 10 cents an hour working 59 hours a week for his father's company, the Blaisdell Machinery Company. Soon he went into the sales department and moved to New York as a machinery salesman. A few years later, he struck out on his own to found the Blaisdell Oil Company with his brother, Walter, in Bradford.

One hot summer afternoon, Blaisdell stepped out on the terrace of the Pennhill Country Club, near Bradford, for a smoke and met a friend lighting a cigarette with a 25-cent Austrian-made lighter. It was a bulky contraption with a brass top that first had to be removed. "You're all dressed

The original 1947 Zippo car. Armed with massive twin lighters towering above its modest roof line, the distinctive car appeared in every major parade in the country in 1948 and 1949. *Courtesy of Zippo Manufacturing Co., Bradford, PA*

up," Blaisdell said to his tuxedo-clad friend. "Why don't you get a lighter that will not make such a bulge in your pocket?"

"Well," replied his friend, "it works."

That retort launched Blaisdell on a new career. He obtained the rights to distribute the Austrian lighter in the United States. He substituted a chrome case for the brass one and raised the price to a dollar. But sales fizzled.

So Blaisdell went back to the drawing board. With three employees sandwiched into a tiny cubicle over a garage, he designed a compact lighter that could be comfortably held in the hand and lit with the flick of a thumb. Even in windy weather, if the flint was good and there was a flammable fluid inside the case, the wick would light. When the wheel was spun against the flint, it made a "z-z-z-z" sound, similar to the zipper on clothing being opened or closed. Blaisdell liked the onomatopoetic ring of the word *zipper*, so he called his new lighter Zippo. Except for some slight modifications on the flint wheel and various advances in the finish on the case, Blaisdell's original Zippo (patent number 2,032,695) is basically the same lighter today.

The Zippo factory is located on Barbour Street in Bradford. Millions of Zippos are manufactured every year in over 30 models ranging from inexpensive versions in brushed chrome to solid gold cases.

NO THANKS!

George G. Blaisdell died in 1978 at the age of 83. For the last 34 years of his life he never smoked, and thus never used his own product.

RUBBING IT IN

Edwin Drake's successful oil rig near Titusville prompted hundreds of men from all over the country to move to northwestern Pennsylvania and make their fortune in oil. Among those who caught oil fever in the late 1860s was Robert Augustus Chesebrough, a 22-year-old chemist from Brooklyn, New York. While hanging around the oil rigs, he noticed that whenever a man got cut or burned he would treat the injury with a colorless residue that formed on the pump rods. The young chemist loaded a keg of the gooey stuff, along with some casks of oil, on a wagon and took them back to his laboratory in Brooklyn.

Chesebrough made hundreds of experiments and finally, in 1870, found a way to extract the wax from crude oil. He called it petroleum jelly. To test its healing powers, Chesebrough scratched and burned his own skin. When he tried to market his discovery, people refused to buy it because its name reminded them of fuel. "It might explode," they exclaimed. So Chesebrough sat down and gave serious thought to a better name:

Crude oil was formed when water in the ground united with hydrogen and carbon. *Wasser* is German for water. *Elaion* is Greek for olive oil. Wasserelaion...vasserlaion...vasserlain... Vaseline!

To market Vaseline, Chesebrough took samples all over Brooklyn and handed them out to construction workers. "If you burn or cut yourself," he advised, "apply this to the injury." They did what he said, and word of the new wonder balm spread quickly.

Chesebrough rented a small factory and went into production. He loaded a wagon with jars of Vaseline, traveled to upstate New York, and gave away samples. Orders trickled in. Next, he hired a dozen salesmen, each with a horse and buggy, and sent them to the New England states. Orders began to multiply.

By 1870, Vaseline Petroleum Jelly, originated in the oil fields of north-western Pennsylvania, was an accepted household remedy. Within a decade, Chesebrough's marketing savvy, combined with the effectiveness of Vaseline, put the wonder jelly into every medicine cabinet from Maine to California.

TO LIFE!

Convinced it was the elixir of life, Robert Chesebrough drank a teaspoon of Vaseline every day. He died in Spring Lake, New Jersey, in 1933, at the age of 96.

THE FIRST SOFT CONTACTS

Dr. Robert Jay Morrison is an internationally renowned optometrist whose office is located at Green and Division Streets in Harrisburg. During the 1960s, he introduced the soft contact lens to the Western Hemisphere.

Morrison first catapulted to prominence in 1957, when he wrote a research paper suggesting that contact lenses might slow the worsening of myopia, or nearsightedness. That article was picked up by several national magazines because myopia afflicts one in every four persons. Patients from all over the world sought out Morrison; his optometry practice burgeoned.

Dr. Robert J. Morrison, who introduced the soft contact lens to North America.
Courtesy of Morrison Associates, Harrisburg

Morrison's article also spurred on the development of contact lenses, which had been moving along rather slowly ever since the advent of plastic lenses during World War II. In 1961, Morrison read of a Czech scientist, Professor Otto Wichterle, who had invented a supple, hydrophilic (water-absorbing) plastic for use in artificial jawbones. Wichterle had commented that the new soft plastic could be suitable for contact lenses. At that time lenses were made from hard plastic, and many wearers found them irritating.

Over the next two years, Morrison made 11 trips to the Czechoslovakian Academy of Science in Prague, and provided his technical and practical expertise in perfecting the soft contact lens. He was present when the prototype soft lens was tried out in 1962.

The Czechs assigned Morrison the exclusive right to develop and market the new lens in the Western Hemisphere. For the next three years, every soft contact lens in the United States was made in his laboratory in Harrisburg. Morrison eventually sold his rights to Bausch and Lomb, a giant American optics firm.

RELIEF FOR CATARACT SUFFERERS

In the 1980s, Robert Morrison, along with ophthalmologist Miles Galin of New York, pioneered a technique in which cataract victims had their cataracts removed and contact lenses installed in a single operation, giving them unprecedented immediate vision.

WE'RE HOOKED!

Born in 1864, Frank Emerson DeLong was always inventing things while growing up in Washingtonville, Montour County. After graduating from

Kelso Academy, he worked in his father's iron foundry in Danville, then sold insurance in Philadelphia. During his spare time, DeLong perfected the folding cardboard box and invented a stenographic machine. And when bobbed hair became the rage in the 1880s, DeLong responded by inventing the bobby pin.

One day DeLong noticed a servant in his house using a piece of twisted wire to close her coat. He improved upon this idea by twisting various thicknesses of wire into an invention he patented as the hook-and-eye fastener. When it was introduced to the public in 1890, sales were phenomenal. Soon there were hook-and-eye factories in Philadelphia and Canada. DeLong built a house on his 600-acre estate in Washingtonville in 1898 and donated funds to improve the town and its school.

THE ZIPPER

Whitcomb L. Judson invented a fastener for footwear in 1891 in Meadville, Crawford County, which he patented under the name "clasp locker for shoes." It consisted of two thin metal chains fastened together by pulling a slider up between them. Thinking his fastener would replace all buttons, hooks, and eyes, Judson teamed up with a friend and promoter named Colonel Lewis Walker. They organized the Automatic Hook & Eye Company and began marketing the Universal Fastener. It did not take hold.

Next, Judson made a more simplified fastener, the C-Curity, which he sold for 35 cents in 1910, to be used not on shoes but on men's trouser flies and women's skirts. C-Curity proved insecure.

Finally, Judson and Walker enlisted Gideon Sundback, a creative Westinghouse engineer who lived in Hoboken, New Jersey. Sundback put together a "separable fastener." The trio formed the Hookless Fastener Company and began to manufacture the item in 1913 in a run-down factory in Meadville.

Sundback's improved version, Hookless #2, gave the company its first big score in 1917, when the United States Navy ordered 10,000 of them for flight suits. The Hookless Fastener Company began to receive orders from manufacturers of all sorts of products across the country. In 1921, the B.F. Goodrich Company ordered 170,000 fasteners for its new galoshes, which the rubber company called Mystic Boots. Then in 1922, a Goodrich executive was dreaming up advertising copy for the company's new boots. He said they just "zip up," so the rubber company registered the word *zipper* as a trademark, and a new word entered our language.

Today, the Hookless Fastener Company is the Talon Division of Textron, which makes all kinds of zippers, including the super-precise zippers for our astronauts' space suits.

BOOK MATCHES

Joshua Pusey of Lima, Delaware County, got the hot idea of putting friction matches into a small folding booklet. Unfortunately, he also put a small strip of sandpaper (the striking surface) *inside* the book. Every time a match rubbed the striking surface while the cover was closed, the entire book caught fire. Three years later, he sold his patent to the Diamond Match Company of Barberton, Ohio, which figured out that the striking surface had to be on the *outside* of the book. The company produced its books of matches, but sales didn't catch fire until 1896, when a Pennsylvania brewery bought 50,000 of them and printed advertisements for its beer on the books—the first such advertisements of their kind.

Around 550 billion matches are manufactured annually, 500 million of which are paper matches in books. Nearly all the matchbooks contain advertising.

FIRST WASHING MACHINES

Two men from Pennsylvania named Smith built the first washing machines. They were not related, nor did they know each other.

Hamilton E. Smith of Pittsburgh was one of the inventors. In 1858, he made a washing machine for his family by attaching two paddles to a wooden tub. The paddles were turned by a hand crank, similar to a butter churn. But his contraption went nowhere because it proved to be harder work than using the common corrugated washboard.

Then there was Stephen Morgan Smith, a Moravian minister from Canal Dover, Ohio. He stopped preaching in 1871 at the age of 32 because of a throat ailment. To make a living, he decided to market a washing machine he had built for his wife some years earlier. The Reverend Smith moved to York County and started to manufacture the "Success." It was the first washing machine to be commercially produced in the United States. Smith made a fortune but gave away most of it to his poorer friends.

Then he started over, this time making a hydraulic turbine. When he died in 1903, his company, the S. Morgan Smith Company of York, was one of the largest turbine manufacturers in the world. It's now owned by Allis-Chalmers.

THE REVEREND'S WASHER

The Reverend Stephen Morgan Smith's washing machine looked like a 50-gallon wooden drum set on its side and mounted on short metal legs. A door was cut on the one side and hinged at the top. A metal rod with paddles ran through the center of the drum and was connected to a geared wheel at one end, and this wheel was connected to another geared wheel. You filled the drum with water, then threw in soap with the laundry. Turning the crank made the paddles turn, which agitated the water, thereby spinning and washing the dirty duds.

The typewriter was invented by Christopher Latham Sholes, who was born on February 14, 1819, in Mooresburg, Montour County. He began his career as a printer's apprentice at the Danville *Intelligencer*. At the age of 18, he moved with his family to Green Bay, Wisconsin.

Sholes became a successful editor, state senator, postmaster, and, finally, customs collector in Milwaukee. In his spare time he experimented in Kleinsteruber's machine shop alongside other aspiring inventors. While trying to invent a machine for serially numbering tickets and book pages, Sholes decided to create a machine that could write every letter in the alphabet as well as numbers. He started by making a gadget that only typed the letter *w*. In 1867, at the age of 48, he succeeded in making the first workable typewriter. It was a clumsy monster with piano-size keys and lots of wires. He used it to type letters to friends and acquaintances, asking them to invest their money in his invention.

One of these letters reached James Densmore, a wealthy businessman in Meadville, Crawford County. Densmore was so intrigued with the contraption that he quickly bought a quarter share of the machine for $600 without even seeing it. Densmore visited Sholes in Milwaukee in March 1868. By that time, Sholes had a second working model of the machine. Densmore advised the inventor, "You'll have to make a dozen more till you get it right."

Over the next three years, Sholes made 50 models (costing $150 each) in an effort to build a perfect typewriter. Densmore, his backer and by then his partner, tried to sell the new writing machine in New York in December 1871, but the business world was not interested. In rejecting the typewriter, most executives explained, "Why should I pay $125 for a contraption to do the work of a pen that costs only a penny?"

Eventually, Densmore approached the Remington Firearms Company in Ilion, New York, which was beginning to diversify from weapons into sewing machines. He convinced the company to manufacture typewriters, and a contract was signed on March 1, 1873. Densmore accepted royalty payments on each typewriter sold. And they must have sold pretty well because he made $1.5 million—a lot of money today but much more back then. Sholes, the inventor, asked for and received a single payment of $12,000 for his patent. With 10 children, it didn't take him long to spend it.

The first five and ten cent store opened in Lancaster, Lancaster County, in 1879.

Frank Winfield Woolworth was born in 1852 on a farm in Jefferson County, New York. When not in school or doing chores on the farm, Frank and his brother Charles Sumner Woolworth played "store." They set up items on the dining table and sold them to nonexistent customers. As a teenager, Frank took a course in storekeeping at a business college in Watertown, but storekeepers turned him down for jobs because he was "too green."

In 1873, at the age of 21, Woolworth got a job as a clerk for Augsbury & Moore, but he had to work for three months without pay to gain experience. When the company became Moore & Smith, it allowed Woolworth to try out his idea of putting up a special counter on which nothing cost more than a nickel. Woolworth's "five-cent counter" repeatedly sold out in a matter of hours.

Early in 1879, Woolworth struck out on his own and opened the world's first "Great 5¢ Store" in Utica, New York. It flopped after four months because of its poor location—on a side street, off the shopper's beaten path. Undaunted, Woolworth moved to Lancaster, Pennsylvania, and opened his Great 5¢ Store on June 21, 1879. Located on a main thoroughfare, North Queen Street just off Market Square, Woolworth's new enterprise was an immediate success. His merchandise moved so fast he had a hard time keeping his shelves stocked with items to sell for a nickel. So he opened up a 10-cent counter. And thus the Lancaster store became the world's first five and ten cent store.

Soon other entrepreneurs picked up on Woolworth's idea and opened their own five and ten cent stores. About a half dozen others opened while Woolworth was expanding into other cities. In 1912, Woolworth bought up five chains of competing stores, becoming the largest merchandiser in the world.

Frank Woolworth died in 1919, and his brother Charles became president of the corporation. His "mother store" in Lancaster closed its doors for good in 1997.

THE WORLD'S (REAL) FIRST TELEPHONE

By a vote of 4 to 3 on March 19, 1888, the U.S. Supreme Court decided that Alexander Graham Bell invented the telephone. Had the vote gone the other way, credit for inventing the telephone would have gone to an eccentric tinkerer from Camp Hill, Cumberland County, named Daniel Drawbaugh.

Drawbaugh was born in a log house on July 14, 1827, in Bloserville, not far from present-day Camp Hill. His father was a blacksmith and a descendant of a long line of mechanics, machinists, and tinkerers. Young Dan followed suit, preferring to work in a shop rather than attend school. He never went beyond fifth grade, but managed to study a dozen or so books on science and mechanics.

Drawbaugh got married and moved to a place along the Yellow Breeches creek at Eberlys Mill. He had 11 children, most of whom were never in good health; only four survived him. He exasperated his wife because he spent more time tinkering in his workshop than earning a living. In debt most of his 84 years, Drawbaugh even had to borrow five dollars to attend his father's funeral. Nevertheless, his neighbors liked him and called him "the wizard."

The Wizard of Eberlys Mill

Drawbaugh called himself an "inventor and designer," but he was also a gunsmith, a piano tuner, and a pretty good mechanic. At the age of 12, he constructed an electromagnetic clock; at 17, he invented a rifle. During his lifetime he received 70 patents. Among his inventions were a carpet rag needle, a weather forecaster, a machine for insulating wire, a paper bag

This was the interior of the workshop of Daniel Drawbaugh, self-proclaimed "inventor and designer." He spent more time tinkering in his shop near Camp Hill than earning a living. Nevertheless, he beat Alexander Graham Bell to inventing the telephone. *Courtesy of the Cumberland County Historical Society, Carlisle, PA*

folder, a steam injector, a stave-jointing machine, an automatic boiler feeder, an automatic fire alarm, a sewing machine, equipment to make wagon wheel rims and barrels, a device to elevate grain in mills, a mowing machine, a coin separator, two stamp cancellers, and an instrument for alphabetic telegraphing.

Drawbaugh also designed a pneumatic stone drill that was used in the construction of the Library of Congress. Despite all these accomplishments, he never earned more than $400 a year for his work. Blame it on his lack of business sense, his inability to promote his talents—and the fact that he had nobody to give him good advice.

By 1860, the telegraph had been around for 20 years, and Drawbaugh was dreaming of ways to send the human voice through its wires. In 1866, he devised an acoustical telephone with a teacup transmitter and a mustard can receiver. When he approached businessmen and bankers in Harrisburg, they showed no interest in his "magnetic talking machine." They wanted to see his designs for improving the use of the telegraph and for a self-measuring molasses faucet.

Along Came Bell

By 1874, Drawbaugh had invented a telephone that worked quite well. At the same time, Alexander Graham Bell and his assistant, Thomas A. Watson, were struggling to get a whisper out of their instrument. The savvy Bell secured a patent on March 7, 1876—three days before his telephone actually worked. Drawbaugh never filed for a patent on his telephone until July 21, 1880. Soon afterwards, he sold his rights to the People's Telephone Company of New York for $5,000 and a large, but never disclosed, amount of stock. Within three months after People's Telephone was up and operating, Bell filed suit against the company in the U.S. Circuit Court of the Southern District of New York. Bell won the case; the court ruled that People's Telephone was doing business in open defiance of Bell's patent.

In those days, public sentiment was against growing corporations and monopolies, and it was obvious that Bell was on his way to building a super-monopoly with his telephone company. In addition, a lot of people were either envious of, or just plain hated, Bell. From 1876 until the end of the century, Bell fought some 600 suits brought by party after party who wanted the U.S. government to strip him of his patents. Thus, People's Telephone Company had a lot of support, both financial and moral, as it appealed the Circuit Court's decision all the way up to the U.S. Supreme Court. The lawyers for People's Telephone brought Drawbaugh to Washington to testify that he actually invented the telephone. To further strengthen their case, the lawyers also produced 70 witnesses, mostly Drawbaugh's neighbors, to testify that Drawbaugh invented the phone in the 1860s. In the end, the court ruled in Bell's favor.

Drawbaugh never appreciated the importance of the telephone, regarding it as a novelty or plaything. He later commented that if he had had $60, he would have filed for his patent ahead of Bell.

By the way, at the turn of the century, Drawbaugh was working on a device to send the human voice over the air without wires. But again, someone else would beat him to it.

THE PRIEST WHO INVENTED THE RADIO

Joseph Murgas was born on February 17, 1864, in Trajov, Slovakia. At 20, he was studying for the priesthood in Ostrihom and experimenting in electricity and wireless telegraphy. Ordained in 1888, he continued his experiments and also became a renowned artist. Most of his paintings were scenes of Slovakian history.

Because of his reputation in the arts, the Hungarian parliament asked Murgas to evaluate a canvas depicting the occupation of Slovakia by the Magyars in A.D. 907. Murgas said it was awful—not at all what the politicians wanted to hear. The legislators made his life so miserable that he left the country and immigrated to the United States in 1896.

Assigned to the Sacred Heart Catholic Church in Wilkes-Barre, Luzerne County, Father Murgas expanded the services of the parish and organized several Slovak societies. The priest had a few hobbies: fishing, collecting butterflies, and painting. In 1898, he built a laboratory in the rectory, where he invented the forerunner of the radio using a rotary spark gap. He called it a "wireless telegraphy apparatus" and obtained a patent for it in 1904.

A group of financiers from Philadelphia known as the Universal Aether Company purchased the patent and planned to market the priest's invention. They spent $25,000 to build two transmission towers, each 200 feet high. One tower stood in Scranton and the other was 19 miles away in Wilkes-Barre. Nothing like these had ever been constructed.

Marconi Beats Him to It

Murgas demonstrated his wireless for some community leaders on April 27, 1905, and it was an astounding success. Among his audience was Navy Lieutenant Commander Sam Robinson, who reported that Murgas' system of wireless transmission would revolutionize world communications, and he recommended that the Navy buy the device immediately. Robinson was promptly informed that the Navy had already contracted to buy radio equipment from a man in Italy named Guglielmo Marconi. Marconi's system could only transmit 15 words per minute, while Murgas' ran 50 words per minute. But the deal was done and the government went ahead with its contract with Marconi.

In 1905, Marconi visited Murgas in Wilkes-Barre and was inspired by what he saw. He admitted, "My experiments in Italy were successful in sending wireless messages across water, but not over land."

"Really," replied Murgas, "I have been sending signals over land for months."

A REEL INVENTOR

Father Joseph Murgas was also an avid fisherman. In 1912, he invented and patented one of the most common accessories for a fishing rod—the casting reel.

Murgas was forced to cut back on his experiments in 1908, when his transmission station in Scranton was destroyed by a storm and two of his financial backers died. Father Murgas went on with his life as a priest. He died in 1929 and was forgotten by the radio industry, but during World War II an American Liberty ship was named after him. Today, a monument in front of the Sacred Heart Church in Wilkes-Barre honors the inventor-priest.

BROADCASTING VOICE AND MUSIC

Both Guglielmo Marconi and Father Joseph Murgas sent the Morse code, a system of dots and dashes, over the air by radio while others were trying to transmit the human voice. On January 1, 1902, Nathan B. Stubblefield of Philadelphia was the first person to send the human voice a distance (one mile) without wires. He was given a patent, but demanded so high a fee for his secret that nobody was interested. Stubblefield stumbled into obscurity.

In 1906, Dr. Reginald Fessenden of the University of Pittsburgh developed the radio telephone, which sent a steady sound wave of voices and music instead of dots and dashes. On Christmas Eve, 1906, he made the first broadcast from Brant Rock, Massachusetts. A man spoke and a violin played "O Holy Night." Fessenden's Yuletide performance went unheralded. His radio system was never sold and his company went bankrupt.

THE FIRST JEEP

World War II was raging in Europe in 1940 and President Franklin Delano Roosevelt realized that the United States could soon be drawn into it. So he directed the military leaders to make preparations. One request came from the infantry for a light cross-country vehicle with a low silhouette, and in response the U.S. Army invited 135 companies across the country to bid on making a quarter-ton vehicle in 49 days. Only two companies responded—Willys Overland and Bantam.

The Bantam Car Company was located in Butler, Butler County. Its factory had been the home of the Standard Steel Car Company in the 1920s until it was purchased by the English Austin Company, which manufactured the "cute and perky" little Austin automobile in Butler. The Austin was particularly popular with movie stars, but that popularity was not enough to keep the company from flopping in 1935.

In 1938, an entrepreneur named Roy Evans took over and renamed the company the American Bantam Car Company. When the bid invitation arrived from the Army in 1940, Frank Fenn, the company president; Harold Crist, the factory manager; and Evans quickly swung into action. Instead of modifying the Bantam car, they designed a vehicle from the ground up. On September 1, 1940, Karl Probst, a Bantam engineer, and Crist personally drove their new vehicle across Pennsylvania into Maryland, and arrived at Camp Holabird in Baltimore ahead of the deadline. The Army called it a General Purpose Vehicle, abbreviated GP—which people shortened to "jeep."

Officials from Willys and Ford were present when the Bantam jeep arrived at Holabird, and they quickly started to make notes. The Army claimed that the jeep project was not patentable, which gave Bantam's competitors free rein to make their own versions. And they did. Ford and Willys knocked out their own jeeps, and the government awarded contracts to all three companies in November 1940. Each would produce 1,500 jeeps.

Unfortunately, the government procurers were afraid that the Bantam Company did not have the capacity to mass-produce jeeps in case of war. Consequently, they gave the big contracts to Ford and Willys. Bantam ended up with contracts to produce trailers instead. The Bantam Car Company remained in business until 1954. Today, there is a Bantam Avenue and a monument to the company in Butler.

Entertaining Times

THE FIRST RE-E-EALY BIG TOP

Englishman John Bill Ricketts was the greatest stunt horseback rider of his day. He came to Philadelphia in 1792, and established a riding school at 12th and Market Streets. There he produced the first real circus in the United States. It was an elaborate show with stunt riders, tight rope dancers, and one clown. Ricketts' show was such a smash that he took it on the road to New York, Boston, and Baltimore. Back in Philadelphia, he built a gigantic white amphitheater and performed on his favorite horse, Cornplanter, named after a famous Indian chief from northwestern Pennsylvania. George Washington was an avid fan of Ricketts', and when the president left office in 1797, Ricketts and Cornplanter gave him a command performance.

RICKETTS' END

George Washington died on December 14, 1799. Three days later, John Bill Ricketts' amphitheater burned to the ground, leaving Ricketts in financial ruin. He gave up in despair and decided to return to England. But he never made it. His ship sank during the Atlantic crossing, and everybody, including the Father of the American Circus, was lost at sea.

THE FIRST AMERICAN-BORN HAM

One of the oldest theaters in the United States is the Fulton Opera House on North Prince Street in Lancaster. On the rear wall of this theater (on Water Street) is a plaque that honors John Durang: "The first native-born American actor, born within sight of this building on January 6, 1768." Actually, that is a mistake. Durang was not the first native-born American actor; he was the first professional dancer born in the United States.

Durang's father, a doctor, moved around a lot, so the boy grew up in Lancaster, York, and Philadelphia. Living near the Southwark Theatre, Durang was bitten early by the show-business bug. His first gig was at the age of 13 in the victory parade following the end of the Revolutionary War. He posed as the god Mercury on a float sponsored by (Ben) Franklin & Hall's Printing Shop. Two years later, an Irish showman named Denis Ryan

The Fulton Opera House on Prince Street in Lancaster was named in honor of the inventor Robert Fulton. A wooden statue of him stands in the niche above the marquee. Behind the Opera House is Water Street, home of John Durang, America's first professional dancer.

On the rear wall of the Fulton Opera House in Lancaster was a plaque honoring John Durang as the first professional actor born in America. He was actually the first American-born professional dancer.

brought his Baltimore troupe of dancers and musicians to Philadelphia. With his father's approval, Durang made a deal with a Mr. Russell, the lead dancer. In exchange for free room and board at the Durang home, Russell would teach young John some of his fancy footwork.

Later that year, Durang ran away from home and joined a theater group in Boston. After three months he returned home. Then Lewis Hallam, the famous showman, heard about the talented youngster and gave him a job in his Hallam Troupe. Thus, Durang began his career as a performer—a dancer, mime, and one-man band.

The First American Theatrical Family

During the first half of the 20th century, one of the most famous theatrical families in the world was the Barrymores of Philadelphia, stars of stage and film. A century earlier, John Durang sired the first family of famous entertainers in this country. Durang married in 1790 and raised a family. He trained his children to be dancers, singers, and musicians, and they toured the country putting on shows. Then the War of 1812 temporarily broke up their act. Too old for military service, Durang put his knowledge of stage pyrotechnics to work by making cartridges for the U.S. military at an arsenal in York.

Durang's sons, Charles and Ferdinand, enlisted in the First Brigade, First Regiment of the Pennsylvania Militia in Harrisburg. In September 1814, the militia marched south to defend Baltimore from an attack by the British. Charles and Ferdinand marched along with their music and instruments in their knapsacks. The militia reached Baltimore after the battle had ended, so the regiment camped on Gallows Hill and waited for three months for the enemy, who never returned. Eventually the Durangs started to look for something to break the monotony, and that's when they made history. Someone brought a newspaper into the camp one day. When the brothers took their turn reading the newspaper, they noticed a poem by a lawyer from Frederick, Maryland. The poem was to be sung to the tune of "Anacreon in Heaven," an English golden-oldie that satirized the virtues of sex, booze, and gluttony. An idea struck Ferdinand. Taking an old volume of flute music from his tent, he looked up "Anacreon in Heaven" and began to play it while his brother sang the words of the poem. Thus, the Durangs were the first people to publicly perform "The Star Spangled Banner."

SLIDE SHOWS

In 1850, two brothers in Philadelphia, W. and F. Langenheim, invented lantern slides, a forerunner of today's slide projector. They began by making positive photos on glass and hand-coloring them. They were usually of people against a painted background. Next, they mounted the glass photos on wire frames and put them in front of a special lens. Behind the lens was a powerful lantern fueled by kerosene that projected the images on a screen or a white wall. The Langenheims came up with a gimmick—the "Top 40" of their day. People paid a special admission to watch shows that were narrative sequences based on popular songs and tales of the time—forerunners of narrative films.

MOVING PICTURE PREDECESSORS

Thomas Edison of New Jersey is recognized as the originator of movies, having taken out a patent on his Kinetoscope in 1889. What is not as well known is that his moving pictures are based in part on a series of inventions by Pennsylvanians that had started to appear 30 years earlier.

The Granddaddy of the Cinema

Coleman Sellers of Philadelphia made the first motion picture projector. The head of a mechanical engineering firm, Sellers was already a successful inventor when he decided, in 1860, to see if he could make pictures move. He posed his two young sons—Coleman Jr. pounded nails in a board while his brother Horace rocked in his little chair next to him. Sellers did not photograph motion; rather, he had each boy move very slightly, then snapped a photo at each move. After he developed all the pictures, he mounted them on a paddle-wheel device. The device was placed inside a drum with a hole from which a tube protruded. A person looked through this viewing tube and turned a crank. This made the pictures flip by in rapid succession, giving the illusion that the children were moving.

Sellers patented his projector on February 5, 1861, and named it the Kinematoscope. Thus, Sellers invented a term that developed into a word that is recognized around the world—*kinema*, or *cinema*.

Hail to Heyl

The next step in the evolution of the movies also took place in Philadelphia. Henry Heyl hailed from Columbus, Ohio, where he was a designer and inventor of machinery. He devised special contraptions to bind books and pamphlets with wire stitching. He also holds the first patent for the wire-stitched paper box that was used by department stores.

Heyl took the Langenheim brothers' lantern shows another step closer to moving pictures with his Phasmatrope, which he first demonstrated exactly four years after Sellers patented his Kinematoscope. First, he photographed a couple dancing. Using a move-and-stop method similar to the one Sellers used, Heyl took 18 pictures of the dancers, then made positives on glass and mounted them on a wheel. The wheel fit around a large cylinder, and inside the cylinder was a powerful lantern. On the cylinder was a hole the size of one glass picture. In front of the cylinder was a projecting lens, and in front of the lens was a shutter that looked like an old-fashioned straight razor. The shutter was attached to a set of gears connected to an axle and a crank. When the crank was turned, the gears moved the glass pictures around the cylinder-lantern while the razor-type shutter in front moved back and forth very fast. Viewers watching the wall on which the image was projected were treated to a movie of people dancing.

Heyl demonstrated his Phasmatrope on February 5, 1870, at the Academy of Music in Philadelphia. An audience of 1,600 saw the dancing couple and then an acrobatic sequence. Heyl took in ticket sales totaling $850.

THE ZOOPRAXISCOPE

In 1878, Eadweard James Muybridge, a professor at the University of Pennsylvania in Philadelphia, took photos of horse races, using dozens of cameras lined up with strings attached to each camera. The strings were stretched across the turf, so when a horse ran over them, the string pulled on a camera's shutter, thereby snapping a picture. Muybridge developed the glass negatives of these photos and then mounted them on a wheel that stood in front of a large lantern and lens. By turning a crank, the wheel revolved so that each picture appeared in front of the light for a fraction of a second and was flashed on the wall. People in the audience got the sensation of watching an actual horse race. Muybridge called his invention the Zoopraxiscope. His exhibition of the Zoopraxiscope at the 1893

Chicago World's Fair was well attended (possibly because it was located next to Little Egypt, the most famous exotic dancer of the day!).

THE FIRST REAL MOVIE DIRECTOR

Throughout the 1890s and early 1900s, the only movies around were the forerunners of newsreels, or performances—magic tricks, dancing, and animal acts. Nobody thought of doing a story with plot and actors. Edwin S. Porter of Connellsville, Fayette County, directed the first *narrative* motion picture—that is, a movie that told a story.

As a young man, Porter left Connellsville to serve in the U.S. Navy as an electrician. Discharged in 1896, he went to New York and worked for the Vitascope film company. He was on hand at Koster and Bial's Music Hall on April 23, 1896, to assist in the first American public projection of motion pictures. Three years later, Thomas Edison hired Porter to work as a mechanic. It wasn't long before Porter began to direct films. He produced *The Life of an American Fireman* in 1902, and *The Great Train Robbery* in 1903. These films were the start of cinematic narrative construction and earned Porter the title "Father of the Story Film."

The Great Train Robbery is also the first film in which the camera moved; it followed the bandits as they made their getaway.

THE NICKELODEON

As movies gained in popularity, businessmen across the country cashed in on the new phenomenon by converting stores into theaters. Since the showing of movies required a large, dark place, these early "theaters" were nothing but dirty, stuffy rooms.

The most significant development in the movie business took place in Pittsburgh on June 19, 1905, when state senator John P. Harris and realtor Harry Davis opened the first "nickelodeon," or five-cent theater, at 433-435 Smithfield Street. It had 96 seats. Among the first films shown were *Poor*

But Honest and *The Baffled Burglar*. They made a profit of over $1,000 in their first week.

The idea quickly caught on and soon Harris and Davis had 14 nickelodeons in Pittsburgh, open from 8 A.M. to midnight, six days a week. The program changed every 15 minutes, allowing the sale of 8,000 tickets per day. By 1910, there were more than 10,000 nickelodeons in the United States.

By the way, Pennsylvania established the first statewide motion picture censorship board in 1911.

IT ALL STARTED HEAR

The world's first commercial radio station, KDKA in Pittsburgh, went on the air on November 2, 1920, and broadcast the presidential election returns.

It all began in 1912 when Dr. Frank Conrad, assistant chief engineer at Westinghouse in Pittsburgh, built a receiver to hear time signals from the Naval Laboratory in Arlington, Virginia. His sole purpose was to win bets on the accuracy of his watch. Conrad enjoyed his hobby so much that he

Dr. Frank Conrad conducted experiments in radio transmission and later supervised the construction of KDKA, the world's first commercial radio station.
Courtesy of KDKA-AM 1020, Pittsburgh

built a transmitter over his garage in Wilkinsburg, a Pittsburgh suburb, and communicated with other ham (amateur) operators across the country.

Bored with ham radio conversation, Conrad decided to play his Victrola (an early record player) into the microphone. This delighted other hams, and soon the world's first disc jockey had a large following of listeners. When people around Pittsburgh learned that they could hear free music on the radio, they began to buy radios. The Joseph P. Horne Department Store in Pittsburgh sold out its entire inventory of surplus radios from World War I, along with the headphones needed to listen to them (these early radios had no built-in speakers).

Many of these wartime radios were manufactured by the Westinghouse Corporation. Conrad's successful broadcasts gave Westinghouse vice president Harry P. Davis an idea: "Let's start our own radio station so we can sell more radios." So in October 1920, workmen constructed a shack on the roof of the Westinghouse factory in East Pittsburgh. Inside, Conrad and fellow engineer Don Little installed a 100-watt transmitter. With the call letters KDKA, it became the world's first radio station—and the first to broadcast a religious service, baseball game, boxing match, and tennis match.

Energizing Firsts

EARLY OIL

During the late 19th and early 20th centuries, Pennsylvania was the largest energy-producing state in the country because of its vast underground reserves of oil and coal.

The Mesopotamians and Babylonians used crude oil in 3000 B.C. The Chinese sent oil through bamboo pipes to heat their homes, but petroleum was first found in vast amounts in western Pennsylvania. On a stream called Oil Creek, in Venango County, during the 18th century, the Indians sopped up oil in blankets, then squeezed it into hollowed-out logs. They used it for medicinal purposes, and the stuff became known throughout the land as Seneca oil.

Oil Salesmen

Rudyard Kipling, the great British novelist, wrote about the first colonist (on record) who sold oil. He was Tobias Hirte, a bachelor who traveled from Philadelphia to the Titusville area in the 1700s. There he stayed several months a year bartering with Chief Cornplanter for crude oil. Seneca oil was supposed to relieve rheumatism, sprains, venereal afflictions, and other ailments. Hirte became the world's first oil franchiser when he bottled the liquid and sold it as medicine. To promote his product, he circulated advertising flyers in German and English. One of these, printed in Chestnut Hill in 1792, told how the Indians gathered petroleum and where it was being sold. He had dealers in Philadelphia, plus Henry Hunsicker in Bethlehem, Dr. Freytag in Easton, William Raab in Reading, Erhard Roos in Lebanon, Sam Saur in Skippack, and others in Maryland.

First Bulk Shipment of Crude Oil

In 1790, Nathaniel Carey collected crude oil in barrels along Oil Creek, transported it in wagons, and sold it to customers in Pittsburgh and throughout the Ohio-Pennsylvania frontier. People who purchased the commodity had unique ideas on how to use the oil. Some tried burning it in lamps, but it gave off an awful odor. Others rubbed the foul-smelling stuff on their horses to keep the flies away.

EARLIEST RECORD OF OIL SALES

General William Wilson kept a general store at Fort Franklin at the confluence of French Creek and the Allegheny River. In his account book for 1797, an inventory of goods shows "3 Kegs Seneca Oil 50 Dllrs." This is the earliest record on the price of petroleum.

SNAKE OIL SALESMEN

In the middle of the 19th century, Americans were being introduced to a new discovery by a group of fast-talking characters with a flair for razzle-dazzle theatrics, known as traveling medicine men. They sold a "remedy of wonderful efficacy that made the lame walk, the blind see..." and could relieve "rheumatism, gout, and neuralgia." A wonder drug? No. Just bottled crude oil, which was found in northwestern Pennsylvania, in territory once occupied by the Seneca Indians—hence the name "Seneca oil."

Many of these hucksters talked so fast that it sounded like they were saying "snake oil." Thus, they became known as snake oil salesmen. With the shortage of doctors, some of these early oil merchants got quite rich!

Bottled crude oil and traveling medicine shows were the brainchild of Samuel Martin Kier, a successful owner-operator of canal boats between Pittsburgh and Philadelphia. He was also in partnership with his father, who had salt wells near Tarentum in Allegheny County. When oil began to seep into the salt, Kier decided to cash in on the old Indian cure-all and he bottled it.

FIRST REFINERY

In 1850, Samuel Kier figured he could get richer if he could find more uses for oil, so he consulted a prominent chemist in Philadelphia who mentioned that, if distilled, crude oil could replace whale oil as an excellent fuel for lamps. Immediately, Kier erected a one-barrel still at 7th and Grant Streets in Pittsburgh. This was the world's first oil refinery. The demand for Kier's "carbon oil" was so great that when Edwin Drake struck oil in 1859, Kier was his first and biggest customer.

THE WORLD'S FIRST OIL WELL

Edwin Laurentine Drake was born in 1819 and spent his childhood in New York and Vermont, but never finished high school. He left home at the age of 19, and worked in a variety of jobs. At the height of the California Gold Rush, Drake was a conductor on the New York and New Haven Railroad, living in New Haven, Connecticut. During the summer of 1857, he became ill and was forced to take a leave from his railroad job. One consolation the railroad had given him was a pass to ride the train for free. This "perk" would land him in the history books.

Drake knew James M. Townsend, president of the City Savings Bank of New Haven and organizer of the Seneca Oil Company, which leased an oil farm near Titusville, Crawford County. Drake was one of the investors in the oil company. Since Drake was on convalescent leave and had a railroad pass, the penny-pinching Townsend asked him to go to Titusville to check out the oil farm. Drake arrived in Titusville in May 1858, and after some testing, he reported back that there was indeed oil on the property.

At age 39, Drake was made general manager of the Seneca Oil Company at an annual salary of $1,000, plus another $1,000 for expenses. Drake hired workmen and had them *dig* for oil. The first thing they hit, though, wasn't oil but a vein of water, and they almost drowned.

After watching a salt-drilling operation near Tarentum, Drake decided to *drill* for oil. He ordered a six-horsepower steam engine and a "Long John" boiler to power the drill. He built an engine house and erected a derrick in which to swing the drilling tools, then installed the engine and boiler.

Drake's Folly

The local folks thought Drake was crazy and dubbed his operation "Drake's Folly." He hired one salt driller after another to run the machinery, but none ever showed up for work. Finally, in the spring of 1859, a blacksmith named "Uncle Billy" Smith took the drilling job for $2.50 per day.

They started to drill in April 1859 alongside Oil Creek, about a mile south of Titusville in Venango County, just off present-day Pennsylvania Route 8. But problems continued to plague Drake's operation. When the drilling started, ground water caused the hole to collapse and clog up. Drake and Smith solved this by getting several 10-foot sections of cast-iron pipe from Erie. They drove the pipes down the hole and sent the drill through the pipes—a method still used today. However, to buy this equipment, Drake used $2,000 of the company's funds, and borrowed another $500 from a bank in Meadville.

The drilling continued for four months, often through solid rock. With the expenses piling up, the Seneca Oil Company decided to cut its losses

A full-size replica of Drake's Oil Well, near Titusville.
Courtesy of the Pennsylvania Historical and Museum Commission

and sent word to Drake to cease all work. But before the letter arrived, something happened.

On Saturday, August 27, Smith and his helpers finished working and looked forward to the next day off. When the machinery stopped, the drill dropped into a crevice 69 feet below the surface, then slipped downward six more inches. The men pulled the drill out of the hole and left the job site for the weekend, not realizing that they had just struck oil.

Eureka!

Smith was a very conscientious guy and never let a day go by without checking on his equipment. Late on Sunday afternoon, August 28, 1859, Smith and his son went to the well site. Smith got down on his hands and knees and peered into the pipe. He saw a dark fluid floating on top of the water within a few feet of the derrick floor. Quickly, he made a long tube with a can on the end and lowered it into the pipe. What he brought up was oil! Excited, Smith's son ran to the nearby mills yelling, "They've struck oil!"

The news spread to Titusville, but Drake did not get to the well until the next day. When he did arrive, he saw Smith busily dipping oil into barrels, tubs, and jars. Drake had drilled the first oil well in the world, making him the father of the modern oil industry. By stubbornly refusing to give in to adversity and continued failures, he succeeded, and what resulted was a boom that made the California Gold Rush look like a garden tea party.

The sleepy village of Titusville soon became a boom town, attracting shady characters, raucous life, loose morals, and dubious democracy. Other towns sprouted up throughout the region, and thousands of wells were sunk. Oil gushed from the pitted earth. An endless chain of wagons loaded with barrels of oil splashed over deep-rutted roads to the nearest railhead.

THE FIRST COMMERCIAL REFINERY

The first commercial oil refinery was erected in June 1860 by William Barnsdall and William Hawkins Abbot in Oil Creek Valley. The only product they produced was kerosene, which they sold for lamps. Their competition was whale oil and rock oil.

GAS MATRICULATION

The first college course on the production of oil and gas was offered by the School of Engineering at the University of Pittsburgh during the 1912–13 term. The instructor was Professor Roswell Hill Johnson.

By Pipe and Rail

As the roads in the region deteriorated, Samuel van Syckel created the first oil pipeline in 1865. This two-inch-diameter pipe carried oil about five miles, from Pithole to the railhead at Miller Farm.

Amos Densmore of Miller Farm devised the first oil tank railroad car. He built two wooden tanks with a capacity of 40 to 45 barrels of oil, and mounted them on a flat car. By the spring of 1866, hundreds of them were in use. These innovations did not sit well with the teamsters, who saw their livelihood threatened. Soon a series of riots and bloody skirmishes broke out between the drovers and the oil operators. The first long-range pipeline was laid across the Allegheny Mountains to the Atlantic coast in 1878.

Epilogue

Six months after he discovered oil, Edwin Drake was let go from the Seneca Oil Company. As severance, the company gave him $1,000, and this entitled them to use his name on their oil barrels. Drake left Titusville in 1863 and soon went broke by speculating in oil stocks that went bad. A victim of neuralgia, he became an invalid for the rest of his life. In 1873, the Pennsylvania state legislature voted him an annual pension of $1,500. Drake died seven years later in Bethlehem. His body was removed to a cemetery in Titusville in 1901.

☞ To Visit: Drake Oil Well Museum

Today, the Pennsylvania Historical and Museum Commission operates the Drake Oil Well Museum on the site of Drake's momentous accomplishment. Outside, visitors can see a full-scale replica of Drake's original well, the largest standard rig ever used in Pennsylvania. A separate building, "one of a kind," houses a unique collection of books, documents, photographs, and artifacts recording the birth and early growth of the petroleum industry. Adjoining Oil Creek State Park offers picnicking and recreation.

Drake Oil Well Museum
RD 3
Titusville, PA 16354
814-827-2797
Hours: Tuesday-Saturday, 9 A.M.-5 P.M.; Sunday, 12-5 P.M.
Closed holidays except Memorial Day, July 4, and Labor Day.
Admission charged.

FILL 'ER UP!

The Gulf Refining Company opened the world's first gas station on December 1, 1913, in Pittsburgh, Pennsylvania. The small structure looked like a Chinese pagoda with an oil can protruding from the top. Located in the center of a triangular plot at the intersection of Baum Boulevard and St. Clair Street, it enabled drivers to enter from the apex of the triangle as well as from both sides.

The Gulf Refining Company opened the world's first drive-in gas station on December 1, 1913. It stood on a triangular plot at the intersection of Baum Boulevard and St. Clair Street in Pittsburgh. *Courtesy of Chevron Corporation*

Gulf hired four men to work in shifts: two to work from 7 A.M. until 6 P.M., the others to work from noon until the station closed at 11 P.M. Thus, at the busiest time of day, noon until 6 P.M., the station had four attendants. Sales on opening day were dismal—only 30 gallons of gas were sold. The next day, things got better when 32 gallons were pumped. The enterprise was off and running by the first Saturday, when 350 gallons were sold. This was enough for W. V. Hartmann, then assistant general manager, to predict, "I am confident that the drive-in station will be more successful than we ever anticipated."

This first station also inaugurated free extras such as free crankcase service, free radiator fill-ups, and free tire inflation. Another "first" introduced at this station was the public restroom.

Along with pioneering free services, this station was the first to institute an eight-hour working day and 24-hour service. A few months after opening, the shift hours were changed to 7 A.M. to 3 P.M. and 3 P.M. to 11 P.M., when the night watchman came on duty.

OPEN ALL NIGHT

One night a car pulled up at Gulf's gas station and the night watchman went outside and was told, "We're almost out of gas. Seeing the light, we thought you might be able to drain enough from the hoses to get us home."

"I'll do better than that," replied the watchman, "I'll fill your tank right up to the top if you give the word." The executives at Gulf learned about the incident and decided it was a good idea. Two days later a sign went up "Open All Night."

The gas station at Baum and St. Clair was so successful that Gulf opened a second at Bigelow Boulevard and the Bloomfield Bridge in Pittsburgh on July 1, 1914. This was followed by stations in Philadelphia and Atlantic City.

WHY STOP FOR DIRECTIONS?

A Gulf employee, William B. Akin, came up with the idea of making road maps, probably to get people to drive more and therefore buy more gasoline. Gulf published and distributed the first automobile road map in 1914. It printed 10,000 maps showing roads and routes in Allegheny County, Pennsylvania.

EARLY COAL

Millions of years ago, most of Pennsylvania was a heavily vegetated coastal swamp. As plants and animals died, they sank into the marshes. The shifting coastal tides poured more plant debris over the partially decayed matter. Through the ages, erosion and landslides added intense heat and pressure, which squeezed the remaining gas and moisture out of this decaying matter, turning it into coal.

FIFTY MORE YEARS

At the present rate of use, the United States has enough coal to last another 50 years, according to Penn State University researchers.

There are two kinds of coal: soft, or bituminous, and hard, or anthracite. Pennsylvania has rich deposits of both types, and this map shows their locations:

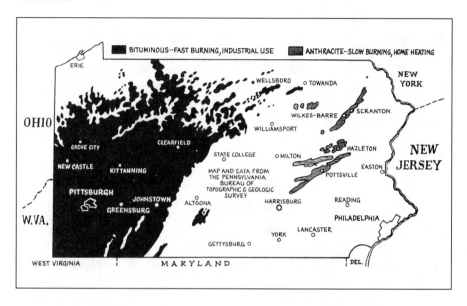

BITUMINOUS

The first coal discovered in Pennsylvania was bituminous. The first traces of it were noted on a map drawn by John Patten about 1752. He noted its location in Westmoreland County, south of the Kiskiminitas River below Saltsburg. In 1759, Colonel James Burd found a vein of soft coal at Brownsville, Fayette County, and burned some of it in his campfire.

The earliest record of actual coal mining in the commonwealth was in 1761 at a mine on present-day Duquesne Heights, across the Monongahela River from what was to become the city of Pittsburgh. This Pittsburgh Vein has been called the most valuable mineral deposit on earth.

The Duquesne Heights mine had two other firsts in the coal industry: the first mine superintendent, James Ed Ward of Fort Pitt, and the first underground mine fire, which started in 1766 and lasted for many years.

ANTHRACITE

Except for a few deposits in Arkansas, Colorado, New Mexico, and West Virginia, nearly all the anthracite in the United States is found in northeastern Pennsylvania. Anthracite contains much carbon, the element that makes diamonds hard. Hard coal generally lies deeper in the earth than soft coal.

INDIANS FIRST

Indians were really the first people in America to use anthracite. Records show that in 1750, an Indian gave some lumps of coal to a gunsmith in Nazareth, present-day Lehigh County, to repair his rifle when the smithy's charcoal ran out.

The real value of anthracite was not fully appreciated at first because the coal was difficult to light and produced such a high heat that it endangered the old-time stoves, which were designed principally for burning wood.

Judge Fell's Experiments

The first use of anthracite for domestic purposes seems to have been discovered by Judge Jesse Fell of Wilkes-Barre, Luzerne County. The following is an excerpt of what he wrote in the introduction to one of his books:

February 11, 1808, made the experiment of burning the common stone coal in the valley in a grate, in a common fireplace in my home and found it will answer the purpose of fuel, making a clearer and better fire at less expense, than burning wood in the common way.

News of Fell's successful experiment spread throughout the town and countryside, and people flocked to see the innovation. Judge Fell's neighbors built their own grates, and soon coal was being used to heat buildings throughout the Wyoming Valley.

THE BEGINNINGS OF THE COAL BUSINESS

Near Wilkes-Barre is the town of Plymouth, where John and Abijah Smith lived. In the spring of 1808, the Smiths loaded two barges with coal and floated them down the Susquehanna to Columbia, Lancaster County, where they tried to sell it. There were no takers, so they left the black stones on the river bank and went back to Plymouth.

The following year, the brothers were ready to try again. They loaded two barges with anthracite, but this time they took along a grate, and headed for Columbia. They set up the grate on shore and burned the coals in it, thus proving the practicability of using coal for heating and cooking. The demonstration was a hit, and they sold all the coal they had, igniting the immense coal trade of Pennsylvania.

THE WORLD'S FIRST ELECTRIC COAL MINE

During the first hundred years of coal mining in Pennsylvania, coal was moved out of the mines on rail cars pulled by mules because steam-powered locomotives would have filled the mines with smoke. That all changed in Landrus, a bituminous mining town in Tioga County. When the Blossburg Coal Company of Tioga County opened the Bear Run Mine in 1887, the owners built a steam-powered plant to generate electricity that would move loaded coal cars on rails in the mine to the top of an inclined plane. There the coal was emptied (or tipped) into the tippler, where it was

THE FIRST COAL IN INDUSTRY

George Shoemaker of Pottsville owned a mine at Centreville. In 1812, he loaded nine wagons of hard coal and headed toward Philadelphia. He sold one wagonload to White & Hazard's Fairmount Nail and Wire Works near Philadelphia, and it became the first factory to burn anthracite in its furnaces. Shoemaker sold a second wagonload to Mellon & Bishop of the Delaware County Rolling Mill. Nobody was willing to buy any of the remaining seven loads, so he simply gave the coal away.

ANTHRACITE IN SMELTING IRON ORE

The Lehigh Coal and Navigation Company used coal in its iron ore furnace at Mauch Chunk, later known as Jim Thorpe, Carbon County, in 1837. Anthracite was used in about 80 percent of the fuel consumed.

The first blast furnace to successfully use anthracite was the Pioneer Furnace in Pottsville, Schuylkill County, which began production on October 26, 1839. Burd Patterson, an early leader in the coal and iron business, owned the land, and he built the furnace in 1838. It was supervised by Benjamin Perry. The furnace produced about 28 tons of foundry iron a week.

separated from rock, crushed and broken, sorted by size, and loaded on trucks or rail cars for shipment to market. The Bear Run Mine operated until 1914. The site is now designated by a stone marker that was dedicated in 1995 by a group of descendants from the town of Landrus.

FIRST NUCLEAR POWER PLANT

The first full-scale nuclear power plant in the United States went on line at Shippingport, Beaver County. Its reactor attained criticality on December 2, 1957, and reached its full capacity of 60,000 net kilowatts three weeks later, on December 2. Its reactor was the same as that used on nuclear submarines. The plant was built by the Atomic Energy Commission and Westinghouse Electric Company on the electrical system of Duquesne Light Company of Pittsburgh.

The Pioneer Furnace was the first blast furnace to successfully use anthracite. It was located on the southern end of Pottsville, Schuylkill County, on "The Island," so called because it was surrounded by the Schuylkill River and the Schuylkill Canal. This photo was taken in 1890.
Courtesy of the Schuylkill County Historical Society, Pottsville, PA

THE FIRST FULLY MECHANICAL COAL MINE

The Butler Consolidated Coal Company started the first fully mechanized coal-mining operation at its Wildwood mine in Wildwood, Allegheny County, in October 1930. The drilling, crushing, loading, screening of sizes, mechanical cleaning, dumping, and transportation operations were accomplished mechanically, with rubber conveyor belts carrying the coal.

The Shippingport plant had an electric output of 60 megawatts electric; thus it could produce power at the rate of 60,000 kilowatt hours—enough to provide electricity for a city of 250,000 people. It consisted of a single pressurized, water-type reactor and its associated systems; four steam generators heated by the reactor; a single turbine generator and associated systems; and a radioactive waste disposal system, along with a laboratory, shops, and administrative facilities. To allow for increased output from future nuclear fuel loadings, the turbine generator was designed with a capacity of one million kilowatts.

President Dwight David Eisenhower broke ground for this power plant by remote control from Denver, Colorado, on September 6, 1954, and formally dedicated the plant by remote control from Washington, D.C., on May 26, 1958. It operated successfully from December 18, 1957, until 1982, when it was shut down permanently.

FIRST ELECTRICAL PLANT OF ITS TYPE

The first three-wire, central-station, incandescent electrical lighting plant in the world was built by the Edison Electric Illuminating Company of Sunbury, Northumberland County, and incorporated on April 30, 1883. The station was constructed by none other than Thomas Alva Edison, who served in the triple capacity of chief electrical engineer, mechanical expert, and superintendent of construction. Edison chose Sunbury as the site of his plant for several reasons: the gas rate of the town was excessive; it was close to the anthracite fields, making fuel comparatively cheap; and the wealthy lumber barons of nearby Williamsport, Lycoming County, were ready to supply the necessary capital for the enterprise.

Wires from the plant at 4th and Vine Streets were strung to the City Hotel, and on July 4, 1883, the switch for the current was thrown. Two 110-volt, direct-current generators were connected in series, raising the distribution voltage to 220 volts. This increase in voltage allowed more current (amperes) to be carried over a given size of wire for a given distance.

Visitors at the Vine Street plant seldom dared to step inside. One is said to have called out to a crowd of the curious, "Come and see the funny bottle with a red-hot hairpin in it that makes light!" The plant was torn down in the late 1930s.

Crime and Punishment

THE CORPORATION COPS

At the turn of the century, there were no state police forces in the United States. The largest police forces were county-wide, usually headed by the county sheriff. The first cops to hold jurisdiction across county lines appeared in the 1860s, when the powerful coal, steel, and rail companies lobbied state politicians for their own police forces. The Pennsylvania General Assembly passed several laws that allowed corporations to establish their own private forces to protect their "rolling mills, collieries, and furnaces."

For a one-dollar fee, a company could obtain a commission from the state to set up its own "coal and iron police force." No training was required to be a corporation cop, so consequently many gunslingers, thieves, and hoodlums, unable to get jobs elsewhere, applied for and became "coal and iron cops." Their abuse of police power was legendary. Most of these cops believed in equality—they harassed and beat up men as well as women, old people, and children.

One of the first attempts by the state legislature to control crime in rural areas was in 1869, when it formed the Spring Valley Police Company. Then, in 1870, the state created the Conneaut Police. The primary job of these two Crawford County forces was to recover stolen horses and other property. In 1872, the General Assembly combined them into the larger State Police of Crawford and Erie Counties—as it is still known today—for the purpose of detecting thieves and recovering stolen horses.

America's First and Finest

In the late 1870s, Pennsylvania was plagued by riots resulting from labor disputes between the railroads and trade unions. The governor called out the National Guard to restore order in Altoona, Pittsburgh, Erie, Philadelphia, Lebanon, Mauch Chunk, Marietta, Meadville, Sunbury, Harrisburg, Shenandoah, Scranton, Wilkes-Barre, Hazleton, and Homestead. These guardsmen were not trained in riot control and as they arrived at Johnstown, the mob opened fire and killed several soldiers.

But the most critical incident occurred in 1902 during the "Great Anthracite Coal Strike." At the village of Lattimer in Luzerne County, striking miners clashed with coal and iron police. Shots rang out and many

The Pennsylvania State Police was the first uniformed police organization of its kind in the United States. One of the first companies was Troop D, located in Punxsutawney, whose members wore "Rough Rider" clothing until their uniforms arrived. Shown in this photo from 1906 are (from left) Charles T. Smith, Henry Hilton, Homer A. Chambers, and George W. Haas.
Courtesy of the Pennsylvania State Police

strikers were killed. The result was a public outcry for an unbiased, well-trained state police force to replace the coal and iron cops. Governor William Stone wanted to hear nothing of it and instead issued 4,512 commissions for coal and iron police to enforce the laws of the commonwealth.

In 1903, Samuel W. Pennypacker was elected governor, which was not good news for the coal and iron cops. He hated them and is on the record as saying, "I will never place police powers in the hands of vested interests. We must have an independent constabulary." On May 2, 1905, the state lawmakers passed Senate Bill 278 and sent it to Pennypacker. The governor promptly signed it, thus creating the Pennsylvania State Police—the first statewide police force in the country.

Superintendent Groome

The first superintendent of the Pennsylvania State Police was Captain John C. Groome, a man with no political interests. Groome had been a successful wine merchant and commanding officer of the First Troop Philadelphia City Cavalry, an Army National Guard unit organized in the mid-1700s. (Its members still wear colonial-era uniforms.) After testing and interviewing many men, Groome selected 200 to serve in four companies located in each section of the state: Troop A—Greensburg, Troop B—Wilkes-Barre, Troop C—Reading, and Troop D—Punxsutawney. Until their blue uniforms arrived, Pennsylvania's cops wore uniforms that resembled Teddy Roosevelt's Rough Riders: cowboy hat, two pistols stuck in the belt, a bandana, and trousers tucked into high boots. (The first female state troopers didn't come on the job until the early 1970s.)

CAPITAL PUNISHMENT

When William Penn founded Pennsylvania in 1681, his Quaker beliefs led him to ban capital punishment in his colony. As a lawyer in England, his

The first superintendent of the Pennsylvania State Police was a man with no political interests. Captain John C. Groome had been a successful wine merchant and commanding officer of the First Troop Philadelphia City Cavalry. *Courtesy of the Pennsylvania State Police*

memories of the death penalty were vivid and horrifying; there were at least 250 offenses that were punishable by death. After Penn died, his commonwealth designated the first crimes that earned the death penalty: murder, rape, burglary, desertion, sodomy, housebreaking, counterfeiting, and robbery. By the 19th century, Pennsylvania had earned the reputation as one of the bloodiest jurisdictions in the United States.

Pennsylvania's last public hanging took place on May 19, 1837, at Bush Hill near 17th and Spring Garden Streets in Philadelphia. Over 20,000 people—half the population of the city—watched the sudden demise of a 19-year-old pirate named James Moran. Public hangings had become a lurid spectacle. Vendors set up booths around the gallows to sell candy, snacks, and liquor; some counties charged admission to watch.

Conditions at these public hangings were often so disorderly that, in 1834, the state legislature ordered the hangings to be held inside the walls of the county prisons. Another problem arose: not all executioners were good at their jobs. Prisoners were often literally *kept hanging* and strangling for up to 17 minutes. Skilled hangmen like William P. Bobb of Lycoming County were in great demand, but they came at a high price. Then the politicians found a cheaper way to mete out the death penalty—electricity.

"Old Smokey"

The cost of holding executions in each of the 67 counties was getting expensive, so the state legislature passed and Governor John Tener signed the act that changed the death penalty to electrocution. The first electric chair was erected in the formidable new prison at Rockview. Situated in Centre County, it was considered the ideal central location. The chair, its electrical system, and supporting apparatus cost the taxpayers $5,000. Prison guards and inmates referred to the deadly device as Old Smokey.

The state also appropriated funds to hire a professional executioner. The first state executioner was Sylvester McNeal. McNeal's first client was John Takap of Montgomery County. He died in the state's new electric chair on February 23, 1915, for killing his young wife.

The Last Electrocutions

The last person to die in the electric chair in Pennsylvania was Elmo Lee Smith. Terrorizing Montgomery County in October 1947, Smith broke into the bedrooms of several women and beat them senseless with anything he could find: a bottle, a stone, a rolling pin, a frying pan, or his bare hands. He was captured, tried, and sentenced to 10 years in the state penitentiary. Shortly after his release, on December 28, 1957, Smith raped and murdered 16-year-old Maryann Mitchell, a junior at Cecilian Academy in Montgomery County. His trial was held in Gettysburg, Adams County, where he was found guilty and sentenced to death. Smith was electrocuted at Rockview Penitentiary on April 2, 1962, the last of 350 people to die this way.

THE STATE EXECUTIONERS

Pennsylvania's executioners did not have happy, peaceful lives:
- Sylvester McNeal, the first, dropped dead of a heart attack in the warden's office after an execution.
- Edward S. Davis resigned and lived as a recluse for the rest of his life.
- After 10 years on the job, John Hulbert shot himself to death.
- Robert G. Elliott watched his house explode.
- The commonwealth hired its own full-time executioner in 1953. Frank Lee Wilson, an electrical engineer from Pittsburgh, got the job. He quit after four years, divorced, became an alcoholic, and died destitute.

THE FIRST ATTEMPT TO KIDNAP A GOVERNOR'S CHILD

Richard Smith had been convicted of killing John Carson, his lover's husband, and the hanging was getting close. His desperate girlfriend, Ann Carson, hatched a plot to kidnap the son of Governor Simon Snyder in the spring of 1816. She went to the prison in Philadelphia where Smith was being held and told him the news. "If Snyder refuses to pardon you, we will kill his son."

Smith's cousin came to visit him, and the convicted killer told him about the plan. The cousin promptly went to the *Democratic Press* offices and spilled the beans to its editor, John Binns. Immediately, Binns dispatched a messenger to Harrisburg to alert his friend, Governor Snyder. And Snyder wasted no time in swearing out a warrant for Ann Carson.

Meanwhile, Carson and her accomplices, Lige Brown and Henry Way, set out from Philadelphia to the governor's home in Selinsgrove. Short on funds, they tried to hold up a freight wagon near Lancaster, but the drover slugged Way, and Carson and Brown took off as the drover ran for help. The sheriff arrived and showed Mr. Way the way to jail. Carson and Brown pressed on with their mission.

Word of Henry Way's capture reached Governor Snyder, who issued orders: "Let them [Carson and Brown] pass through Harrisburg, then arrest them."

A few days later, Way slugged a prison guard, nearly killing him, and escaped. He was never heard from again. Carson and Brown traveled through Harrisburg and continued north to Clarks Ferry, at the confluence of the Susquehanna and Juniata Rivers. They checked into a hotel and went to their room. That night, the militia surrounded the building, closed in, and captured the would-be kidnappers.

Carson was held in Harrisburg on $5,000 bail. Despite all her efforts, her lover, Richard Smith, was hanged. After friends paid her bail, Carson fled to Philadelphia and joined a counterfeiting ring. While trying to pass phony money at the Girard Bank, she was busted. She was sentenced to the Walnut Street Prison and worked in the infirmary there. Carson contracted typhoid fever while nursing other prisoners suffering from the plague. She died on April 27, 1817.

Politically Speaking

OUR FIRST WOMAN GOVERNOR

William Penn, founder of Pennsylvania, died at the age of 74 on July 30, 1718, in the family's home near Reading, England. His second wife, Hannah Callowhill Penn, inherited Pennsylvania's 28 million acres of land, thus becoming governor of the province. At the time, the commonwealth's population of 46,000 lived in three counties—Bucks, Chester, and Philadelphia, the latter with a quarter of the population, numbering some 10,000 citizens.

In reality, Hannah had been running the commonwealth since William suffered a mild stroke on October 4, 1712, which left him partially paralyzed. He was unable to speak or sign his name, so Hannah took charge. Her financial savvy also saved Pennsylvania from bankruptcy. Here's how it happened.

William Penn had a steward, Philip Ford, who handled the finances of the colony, including sales of land. Ford charged exorbitant commissions and squandered thousands of British pounds, and soon the colony had a £10,500 debt. Ford took advantage of Penn's trusting nature by telling him that the colony was in a financial bind and they had to take out a loan to pay the creditors. Penn signed a paper, which turned out to be a deed of conveyance, making Ford the owner of Pennsylvania if Penn did not personally pay the colony's creditors.

Ford died and his widow and children sued in 1708. William Penn, then in his sixties, could not pay, so he was arrested and thrown in jail. During the next three years, Hannah Penn called on her fellow Quakers, who raised £7,600. The Ford family accepted this as settlement and William was released from prison.

Born to Business

Hannah was born in Bristol, England, in 1671. Her father, Thomas Callowhill, was a businessman in international trade. Growing up, she learned from her parents the science of marketing and accounting. At the age of 24, Hannah became the second wife of widower William Penn, who was 54 at the time. Penn viewed Hannah's good business sense as one of the many qualities necessary in a woman who would accompany him to America and be a stepmother to his three young children.

During Hannah's tenure as governor, she paid off the mortgage on the colony along with other lingering debts. Upon her death on December 20, 1726, she left a solvent Pennsylvania to her children.

PENNSYLVANIA'S FIRST GOVERNOR

The first popularly elected governor of Pennsylvania was Thomas Mifflin, one of the Founding Fathers of the United States. With the possible exception of Benjamin Franklin, no other Pennsylvania politician had as far-ranging a career as Mifflin: local councilman, a brigadier general in the Revolutionary War, president of the Continental Congress, president of Pennsylvania, and presiding officer at the convention that drew up the state constitution of 1790.

Mifflin was born in Philadelphia on January 10, 1744. His father was a wealthy merchant who had been a trustee of the College of Philadelphia, now the University of Pennsylvania. Mifflin graduated from that institution in 1760, then worked for the countinghouse (accounting firm) of William Coleman. Five years later, Mifflin went into the mercantile business with his brother.

Mifflin was raised a Quaker, a religion that promotes pacifism. When he joined the army during the Revolutionary War, he quit the Society of Friends. Mifflin was about five feet eight, of athletic build, cheerful, handsome, and an eloquent speaker. As a young man, he was a radical, demanding freedom for the colonies and a war with Great Britain, if need be.

In 1771, at the age of 27, Mifflin entered politics as one of six wardens of Philadelphia. A year later, he was elected to his first of four successive terms in the Pennsylvania Assembly. The legislature selected him as a delegate to the First and Second Continental Congresses, where he was one of the youngest and most radical members. When word reached Philadelphia that shooting in Lexington and Concord, Massachusetts, had ignited the Revolutionary War, Mifflin campaigned to get Pennsylvania into the fray. His most famous oration was made at a town meeting in late April 1775:

> Let us not be bold in declarations, and afterwards cold in action.
> Let not the patriotic feelings of today be forgotten tomorrow, nor
> have it said of Philadelphia that she passed noble resolutions,
> slept upon them, and afterwards neglected them.

Mifflin practiced what he preached. He immediately joined the Continental Army. On May 19, 1776, Congress commissioned him a brigadier general and he was given command of the Pennsylvania Line. After the war, in 1783, Mifflin was elected to Congress and was soon elevated to president, the highest position in government under the Articles of Confederation. In fact, it was to Mifflin that General Washington submitted his resignation from the army. During that same presidency, Mifflin signed the peace treaty with Great Britain.

President of Pennsylvania

Mifflin represented Pennsylvania at the Constitutional Convention of 1787, and he signed his name to the Constitution of the United States of America. The following year, he was chosen as a member of the Supreme Executive Council of Pennsylvania and, toward the close of the year, when Benjamin Franklin retired, he was elected president, meaning president of Pennsylvania. In 1790, Mifflin helped rewrite the state's constitution, which replaced the executive council with a governor who would serve a three-year term, not to exceed three terms. For the first time in the state's history, its chief executive—the governor—would be elected by the people.

Won by Landslides

When the election was held, Mifflin defeated the conservative candidate, General Arthur St. Clair, 27,725 votes to 2,802. Mifflin ran for two more terms: In 1793, he defeated Congressman Frederick A. Muhlenberg, 19,590 votes to 10,700. In 1796, he won by a landslide; garnering 30,020 votes, he clobbered both Muhlenberg and General "Mad Anthony" Wayne, who could only muster a total of 1,149 votes.

IN HOT WATER

The Hot Water War (also known as Fries' Rebellion) was an uprising by eastern Pennsylvanians against the federal real estate tax. At that time, a house was assessed according to the number of windows it had. Windows were expensive then, and the more a house had, the greater was its assessed value. The Hot Water War was so called because people dumped hot water on window-counting revenue agents. Governor Mifflin called out the militia from Reading, Berks County, in 1798, and the troops marched into Lehigh County and arrested the rebels.

As governor, Mifflin purchased the 202,000-acre Erie Triangle for 75 cents an acre and sought public health improvements to curb yellow fever epidemics. During his tenure, the state capital was moved from Philadelphia to Lancaster.

THE BEGINNINGS OF PATRONAGE

Thomas McKean of Londonderry, Chester County, was the second governor of Pennsylvania. Elected in 1800, he served three stormy terms, caused partly by the fact that he started the patronage system in Pennsylvania politics as soon as he was elected. While his predecessor, Thomas Mifflin, had tolerated both Federalists and Democrat-Republicans, McKean quickly adopted the doctrine of "to the victor belong the spoils." In a letter to President Thomas Jefferson in July 1801, McKean wrote, "It appears that the anti-Republicans, even those in office, are as hostile as ever....To overcome them they must be shaven, for in their offices (like Samson's hairlocks) their great strength lieth."

McKean's purpose in removing opponents was not merely to make places for his political cronies, but "to secure efficiency and harmony to his rule." Once his power was secured, he deviated from his patronage policy, and appointed political adversaries if they could greatly benefit his administration.

The Political Moonlighter

McKean, born on March 19, 1734, the son of an immigrant Irish tavern keeper, had an impressive 50-year career in politics, holding elected office in two states at the same time. He began as a prothonotary in Delaware, then became deputy attorney general there. In 1757, at the age of 23, he was elected clerk of the Pennsylvania Assembly. For the next 25 years, he divided his time between Delaware and Pennsylvania. At times, his career was downright confusing.

As a lawyer in 1762, McKean codified the Pennsylvania Assembly's laws on appointments. That same year, he was elected to the first term of his 17 years in the Delaware legislature. During his last six years in the Delaware Assembly he lived in Philadelphia.

During the Revolution, McKean served as a colonel in the Pennsylvania Line and was almost killed in action in New Jersey. In 1777, he was named chief justice of the Pennsylvania Supreme Court, holding that post for 22 years. Simultaneously, McKean was an elected member of the Delaware Assembly and was a congressman from Delaware. For two months in 1777, he was even president of the Delaware Assembly.

McKean was the only future governor of Pennsylvania to have signed the Declaration of Independence. He was president of Congress from July 10 to November 5, 1781.

McKean was tall, dignified, and brilliant, but he was also haughty, vain, and tactless. And he had a greedy obsession for power. He was elected governor three times: in 1799, 1802, and 1805. His domineering personality made for a contentious administration. McKean's enemies multiplied and he faced an attempted impeachment, which died in legislative committee. He constantly fought with the press, vetoed bills, and saw his requests, such as free public education, ignored. Consequently, he bombed as governor.

The single major development during McKean's tenure as governor (1800 to 1808) was the formation of a record 16 counties in the northwestern part of the state. McKean County is named after him.

THE FIRST WORKING-CLASS GOVERNOR

Simon Snyder was born on November 5, 1759, in Lancaster, one of five children of immigrant German parents. His father was a mechanic and died when Simon was 15. He went to York to attend night school and learn the trade of tanning during the day. Extremely ambitious, Simon moved to Selinsgrove at the age of 25, where he ran a store and a mill, and served as justice of the peace for 12 years. He was self-educated, modest, friendly, and a popular politician because he refused to give long speeches.

Snyder was a delegate to the Pennsylvania Constitutional Convention of 1790. He was elected to the state house of representatives in 1797. He served 11 years and was twice speaker. He was a political leader of the rural population in Pennsylvania, which, at the turn of the 19th century, was increasing in great numbers.

Snyder ran for governor four times. In 1805, he lost his first attempt to Governor McKean, 43,644 votes to 38,483, but he proved to be a strong contender. He ran again in 1808 and beat former U.S. Senator James Ross, a Federalist from Pittsburgh. Snyder, 49, and a self-acknowledged "commoner," refused to have any inaugural ceremony.

During Snyder's administration (1809 to 1817), eight counties were formed, the office of auditor general was created, and the state established free education for paupers. The state capital was moved to Harrisburg, Dauphin County, making Snyder the first governor to serve in the new capital city. Another important milestone for Snyder is that he was the first successful leader of the new Democrat-Republican Party, which controlled Pennsylvania politics for 48 of the 52 years until the Civil War.

After Snyder left the governorship, he won a term in the state senate and is the only governor to return to that legislative body. His tenure as a senator did not last long. After 23 months in office, Snyder caught typhoid fever and died on November 9, 1891, at the age of 60. In 1881, the legislature appropriated $3,000 for a monument at his grave in Selinsgrove, the county seat of Snyder County, the third and last county named after a governor.

THE FIRST—AND ONLY—U.S. PRESIDENT BORN IN PENNSYLVANIA

The only native son of Pennsylvania to occupy the White House was James Buchanan, our 15th president, who served from 1857 to 1861. Just like Presidents Andrew Jackson, James Knox Polk, and Millard Fillmore before him, Buchanan was born in a log cabin—on April 23, 1791, the second of 15 children, on a farm called Stony Batter near the village of Cove Gap, Franklin County. Part of this cabin is on display in Mercersburg. As a small boy, Buchanan used to wander around his home with a bell tied around his neck so his mother could hear where he was at all times.

Buchanan attended Dickinson College in Carlisle, Cumberland County. To gain acceptance by his schoolmates, he admitted, "I engaged in every sort of extravagance and mischief." The college expelled him for disorderly conduct, but on his promise to behave, readmitted him. Buchanan graduated in 1809 with highest honors. He moved to Lancaster and studied law with James Hopkins. Three years later, at the age of 21, he was admitted to the bar.

At the outbreak of the War of 1812, Buchanan enlisted, and after his honorable discharge, Private Buchanan went into politics. In 1814, he was elected to the Pennsylvania legislature. From 1821 to 1831, he served in the U.S. Congress.

Ambassador, Senator, and Secretary

In 1831, President Andrew Jackson appointed Buchanan U.S. ambassador to Russia. At St. Petersburg, he worked out a commercial treaty that allowed American ships to trade on the Baltic and Black Seas. He returned home in 1833, ran for the U.S. Senate, and won. As senator from Pennsylvania (1834 to 1844), Buchanan achieved a reputation as an orator and logician. President James Polk, whom he had helped in carrying the doubtful state of Pennsylvania, appointed him secretary of state in 1845. His most notable accomplishment in this job was avoiding another war with Great Britain over the northern boundary of the Oregon Territory. Buchanan ended the crisis in 1846 with a straight-line U.S.-Canadian boundary from Minnesota to the Pacific. When Franklin Pierce became president in 1853, he appointed Buchanan ambassador to Great Britain.

President Buchanan

Buchanan had tried three times to win the Democratic nomination for president—in 1844, 1848, and 1852. He finally won the nomination on his fourth try in 1856. His main opponent in the general election was the candidate of the newly formed Republican Party, John C. Fremont. Former president Millard Fillmore was the candidate of the anti-Catholic, anti-immigrant "Know Nothing" party. Buchanan won only a minority of the popular vote, but he trounced his opponents where it really counted, in the electoral college. It should be noted, however, that Buchanan carried his home state of Pennsylvania by just 3,000 votes. His main support lay in the

One of the few statues of President James Buchanan in existence stands in Buchanan Park, on Wheatland Avenue in Lancaster.

South; he had carried every southern state. As president, Buchanan considered slavery a moral wrong, but felt that it must be upheld where it existed, and that citizens of territories about to become states should decide for themselves whether or not to permit slavery.

WHITE HOUSE HOSTESS

When Buchanan became president, his niece, Harriet Lane—a statuesque blonde with violet eyes—lived with him in the White House and acted as his official hostess. For almost his entire administration, Harriet was more popular than her president-uncle. A steamboat was named after her. The well-known song "Listen to the Mockingbird" was one of dozens of popular entertainments dedicated to her.

Bachelor President

Twenty-seven-year-old James Buchanan was a rising attorney in Lancaster and one of the city's most eligible bachelors when, in 1818, he attended one of the gala soirees at the White Swan Inn. There he met Ann Coleman, the belle of the ball and daughter of one of the richest men in the country—Robert Coleman, owner of iron foundries from Hopewell Furnace to Martic Forge. It was love at first blush, and James and Ann became engaged. This didn't please Ann's parents, who disliked Buchanan.

As their courtship blossomed, so did Buchanan's business. His case load was filled with lawsuits stemming from the financial panic of 1819. He was also preoccupied with his job as state representative in Harrisburg. The busier he got, the less time he spent with Ann. This caused the bluebloods of Lancaster to speculate that Buchanan did not love Ann as much as he loved her daddy's money.

The break-up came when Buchanan returned from a lengthy business trip and stopped to visit friends before calling on Ann. Staying with his friends was an attractive and available young woman named Grace Hubley. When Ann Coleman heard about this, she went into a jealous rage and wrote a note to Buchanan calling off the engagement. Buchanan received the note while in court. He read it, blanched, recovered, and went right on working. He felt that because of Ann's large fortune, it was useless to do anything to try to win her back. As the days wore on, Ann became more and more broken-hearted over not hearing from Buchanan. Her family sent her to stay with relatives in Philadelphia for a change of scenery. Two days later, Ann Coleman, age 22, suffered a fit of hysteric convulsions and died.

LARA THE POOCH

President Buchanan had a Newfoundland dog named Lara, which was famous for his immense tail and strong attachment to his master. An anecdote about Lara involves the "Bleeding Kansas" crisis. In 1857, politicians in Kansas Territory held a convention in the town of Lecompton to write a state constitution, but they faced a stumbling block: Should they or should they not legalize slavery in the territory? Eventually, the Lecompton convention passed a no-slavery constitution and sent it on to Washington. Buchanan forwarded it to Congress with the recommendation that Kansas be admitted into the Union. This embittered the southern congressmen, so they voted against it. For many complex reasons, the northern Democrats, Free-Soilers, and Republicans also voted it down. Kansas was denied statehood, and Buchanan was left feeling quite embarrassed.

Afterwards, if any strangers ever walked into the White House, Lara would stand up, shake himself from head to foot, and eye the stranger fiercely "as if he were a thief or an anti-Lecomptonite." The dog stayed that way until the stranger said in a loud voice, "Lecompton," upon which Lara immediately resumed his dozing attitude, one eye shut, the other half open.

Lost to Lincoln

In trying to please both slavery advocates and slavery abolitionists, Buchanan ended up pleasing nobody. He was so unpopular that he decided not to seek his party's nomination in 1860. Senator Stephen Douglas of Illinois won the Democratic nomination for president in 1860, leaving Buchanan as a lame duck leader. When Abraham Lincoln, an outspoken slavery opponent, won the presidential election in November, the southern states began to secede from the Union. In his last State of the Union message early in 1861, President Buchanan said, "The southern states have no right to secede, but Congress has no power to make them stay in the Union....I only want to keep peace until President Lincoln takes over...."

Buchanan left office on March 4, 1861, and retired to Wheatland, his estate on Marietta Avenue in Lancaster. He died there on July 1, 1868.

☞ To Visit: Wheatland

Wheatland, the historic residence of President James Buchanan, has been restored to capture the splendor of the period of Buchanan's ownership from 1848 to 1868. Visitors can view a variety of Victorian period rooms, as well as the president's study filled with original furnishings, books, and decorative objects. The building is situated today on more than four acres of land containing centuries-old trees. Visitors are free to wander leisurely around the grounds. Tours of Wheatland are given by well-informed guides in period-style costume.

Wheatland

1120 Marietta Avenue
Lancaster, PA 17603
717-392-8721
Hours: April 1-November 20: daily except Thanksgiving, 10 A.M.-4:30 P.M. Admission charged. Special group rates are available, but call for an appointment. Special Christmas candlelight tours are held in early December; call for exact dates and hours.

Wheatland, the home of James Buchanan, the first (and only) president of the United States born in Pennsylvania. His estate stands on Marietta Avenue near President Avenue in Lancaster and is open for tours.

THE FIRST AND ONLY FOREIGN-BORN GOVERNOR IN THE 20TH CENTURY

John Kinley Tener was born in County Tyrone, Ireland, on July 25, 1863. His father died 10 years later, and soon his mother moved her family of 10 children to America and settled in Pittsburgh. She died that same year, 1873, and Tener was left an orphan.

Nevertheless, he graduated from high school in Pittsburgh, attended business college, and worked as a paymaster. In his spare time, Tener played baseball. A scout spotted him and recruited him into the New England League. Next, he pitched for the Chicago Cubs in 1888 and 1889. His short professional career ended with the Pittsburgh team in 1890. Tener is the only professional athlete to be governor of Pennsylvania.

Tener settled in Charleroi, Washington County, and became a cashier of the First National Bank. A few years later, while still a young man, he was promoted to bank president. An active member of the Elks, he became its Grand Exalted Ruler in 1907. The following year, he entered politics and was elected to Congress. In Washington, D.C., he stayed in the same hotel as Pennsylvania's U.S. senator, Boise Penrose. In 1910, Penrose wielded his powerful influence in getting Tener elected as the Republican candidate for governor.

Tener ran in November 1910 against a Democratic candidate and another opponent from the Keystone Party, consisting of independent Democrats and Republicans. Tener won the election with the lowest percentage of votes in Pennsylvania's history.

Surprisingly, Tener proved to be a progressive and probably the most underrated governor of the first half of the 20th century. His administration had many accomplishments: a $4 million highway bill was passed to improve the state's poor highways; the Pennsylvania Historical and Museum Commission was established; the Education Code of 1911 was passed, creating the Council of Education, which provided the first schooling for the mentally handicapped; the licensing of hunters began; the Uniform Primary Law of 1906 was put into effect in 1914, providing the first primary elections. The commonwealth began to purchase the normal schools—state teachers colleges—from private owners, thus creating the state university system. During the last two years of his governorship and until 1918, Tener was president of the National Baseball League—the only Keystone State governor ever to hold that office.

Tener's name was entered in the GOP primary for governor in 1926. Without ever campaigning, he finished third. He retired from politics and spent his last years as a successful businessman in New York City and Pittsburgh.

Schools, Churches, and Architecture

THE FIRST TEACHERS IN PENNSYLVANIA

Before William Penn became the proprietor of Pennsylvania, the colony was under the control of the Dutch as part of New Netherland. The first known schoolteacher was Evert Pieteson, a Hollander who was employed by the colonial government to act as schoolmaster and *zieken-trooster* (comforter of the sick), "to read God's Word and to lead the singing upon the arrival of the clergyman." There is some evidence to show that, a little later, a number of schoolmasters traveled from home to home.

SUED FOR BACK WAGES

The records of Upland Court show that on March 22, 1679, Edmund Draughton sued Duncan Williams for 200 guilders as wages for teaching Williams' children to read the Bible. The teacher won the suit.

THE FIRST LAW FOR EDUCATION

William Penn was a strong advocate of education for all. In March 1683, the Provincial Council followed his suggestion by adopting the Second Frame of Government, or Great Law, which included this provision:

To the End that Poor as well as Rich may be instructed in good and Comendable learning...persons in this Province and territories thereof, having Children, and all the Guardians or Trustees of Orphans, shall cause such to be instructed in Reading and Writing...[It further provided that] The Governor and Provincial Council shall erect and order all public schools.

Penn's Frame of Government also provided the first vocational education patterned after the apprentice system in England:

All children within this province of the age of twelve years shall be taught some useful trade or skill, that the poor may work to live and the rich, if they become poor, may not want.

THE FIRST SCHOOLS

Unfortunately, after Penn died, the colony's political leaders ignored public education. For the next century, practically all schools in the colony were established and run by religious groups.

An outstanding teacher in early Pennsylvania was Christopher Dock, "the pious Schoolmaster on the Skippack," in Montgomery County. He was a Mennonite and a farmer as well as a schoolmaster. For more than half a century, from 1714 to 1771, his school was an educational showplace. While most schoolmasters ruled their students with an iron fist, Dock ruled his by the law of love.

Many English-speaking religious groups established schools. The Anglicans founded Christ Church in Philadelphia in 1695 and attached a school to it. The Baptists built their first church at Cold Springs, Bucks County, in 1684 and established several church schools in southeastern Pennsylvania. The first Roman Catholic church in Pennsylvania, St. Joseph's, was established in 1730 in Philadelphia and it, too, had a school.

The Scotch-Irish were possibly the most active group when it came to schooling, especially on the Pennsylvania frontier. Scotch-Irish ministers, followers of the Presbyterian Church, started some of the first elementary schools in the country. The most noted school was the classical academy established by the Reverend William Tennent in Bucks County in 1726, popularly known as The Log College. Another classical school at New London, Chester County, was founded in 1741 by the Reverend Francis Alison.

Neighborhood and Subscription Schools

As British culture spread into central and western Pennsylvania, another type of school appeared—neighborhood schools. These were usually held in the home of a mother who taught her children along with some of the neighbors' offspring.

Next came subscription schools. Local citizens raised money to build a schoolhouse and pay a teacher, and attendance was by tuition. If you couldn't afford to pay, your children weren't allowed in. The first school west of the Alleghenies was of this type, established in Pittsburgh in 1759.

PENNSYLVANIA'S FIRST FREE PUBLIC SCHOOL SYSTEM

The state's constitutions of 1776 and 1790 called for the legislature to provide free schooling throughout the commonwealth for the poor. It got nowhere because of a law passed in 1802 that instructed local officials to identify all the poor people in their area. In those days, hardly anyone would admit to being poor.

By 1830, almost every northern state had a better system for free public schools than Pennsylvania. Meanwhile, middle-class workers, some farmers, and the progressive rich were clamoring for better schools.

The Free School Act

In 1832, George Wolf won election to a second term as governor. A plank on his campaign platform advocated free public schools statewide. After a two-year struggle, the General Assembly finally passed, and Wolf signed, the Free School Act on April 1, 1834. The act is the foundation of today's Pennsylvania public school system. It designated each county as a school *division*, and each township, borough, and city ward, a school *district*. A district could draw on state school funds only if it voted to have free schools and levied a school tax. Half of the districts rejected the whole idea. Many Pennsylvania Germans saw public schools as a threat to their language and culture, and religious groups wanted to maintain control so that they could educate their offspring in their own faith. Others resented paying taxes to educate somebody else's kids. All these groups put pressure on their representatives to repeal the act.

When the repeal came up for a vote, Representative Thaddeus Stevens of Adams County gave the most rousing speech of his career and convinced his colleagues to back Governor Wolf on free education. Thanks in great part to Stevens, the Free School Act was saved.

Training Teachers

With the passage of the Free School Act, schools sprang up all over the commonwealth, and there weren't enough teachers to go around. Lancaster County came up with a solution: It established the Lancaster County Normal School in 1855, the first teachers college in the commonwealth. (In the mid-19th century, a normal school was a two-year teachers college.) The founders wanted to put the school in Strasburg, but the townspeople refused to have it. The scholars looked elsewhere and found a site in Millersville. Two years later, the state legislature passed the Normal School Law and designated the Lancaster County Normal School in Millersville as Pennsylvania's first state normal school.

The commonwealth took ownership of the college in 1917. Millersville became a state teachers college in 1928, and a state college for liberal arts and education in 1960. Since 1983, it has been Millersville University of Pennsylvania, part of the State System of Higher Education.

THE FIRST LAND GRANT COLLEGE IN PENNSYLVANIA

Penn State, Michigan State, Ohio State, the Universities of California, Illinois, Texas, Washington, and many others are land grant colleges and universities. These institutions receive funding from both the state and federal governments. Pennsylvania State University in State College, Centre County, owes its origin to a casual conversation between attorneys Fred Watts of Carlisle, Cumberland County, and H. N. McAllister of Bellefonte, Centre County. In the early 1850s, higher education was limited to the rich who wanted to study law, medicine, and theology. Watts and McAllister discussed the need for a "college to train farmers' sons in agricultural science."

The lawyers brought their idea to Governor William Bigler, who gave it his wholehearted support. Next, they addressed the state agricultural society convention on January 18, 1853, and urged the society to start an "institution to teach agricultural science." After the society endorsed their concept, Watts and other members drew up a charter for establishing the Farmers High School of Pennsylvania. The state legislature approved the charter, and Governor Bigler signed it in April 1854.

A location was needed for the school, so in July 1854, its trustees placed advertisements in newspapers across the state, asking landowners to donate some of their property. Offers came from landowners in Blair, Centre, Erie, and Franklin Counties. The trustees chose a site donated by General James Irvin of Centre County, because it was located near the geographical center of the state, and because Irvin, McAllister, and a criminal lawyer/politician named Andrew Curtin—all of Bellefonte—donated $10,000 each to the new school.

Farmers High School

Farmers High School opened in 1859 with an enrollment of 119 students. The first president of the school was Dr. Evan Pugh. Born in Chester County and educated in Germany, Pugh worked 18 hours a day to organize courses of study and keep the place from going bankrupt. One night, while returning from a business trip, Pugh was thrown from his horse and fell down an embankment near Bellefonte, about 10 miles north of Farmers High School. He never recovered from his injuries and died before his 36th birthday.

In 1860, Farmers High School was renamed the Agricultural College of Pennsylvania. The following year, the Civil War broke out, and with reduced enrollment the college hit financial hard times. During the war, in 1862, President Lincoln signed the Land Grant Act, which granted every state 30,000 acres for each senator and representative it had in Washington. The land was to be sold, the proceeds invested, and the income used to create and maintain a college for agriculture and the mechanical arts. The Agricultural College of Pennsylvania was designated as the commonwealth's land grant college.

After the war, the college began to grow and prosper. The town around the college was named State College, and in 1874 the school's name was changed to Pennsylvania State College. It was designated Pennsylvania State University in 1953.

LEARNING BY MAIL

The Pennsylvania legislature passed a law in 1885 that required anyone who wanted to be a mine foreman to take an examination and be certified. At the time, few miners could afford to leave their jobs to attend college, let alone pay the tuition. A newspaper editor came up with the solution.

Thomas Jefferson Foster, from Pottsville, Schuylkill County, owner/editor of the Shenandoah *Herald*, went on to publish the *Colliery Engineer*, which had a questions-and-answers column on mining problems. Bombarded with questions from aspiring mine foremen, Foster came up with the idea of starting a correspondence course in mining, and the first student was registered in 1891. Within six months, over 1,000 men were studying the fundamentals of mine development and operation at their kitchen tables. Foster was soon faced with a demand for more courses in other skills. Over the years, he added more than 300 courses in a host of skills and trades. The International Correspondence School, which Foster advertised as the "World Schoolhouse," was headquartered in Scranton, Lackawanna County. It is recognized as the first correspondence school.

THE FIRST AMERICAN MALE SAINT

Only three Americans have become saints, and two were women: Mother Frances Cabrini and Mother Elizabeth Seton. The third was Bishop John Neumann, archbishop of Philadelphia from 1852 until his death in 1860.

John Neumann was not an impressive-looking man. Full grown, he was less than five feet, four inches tall, and was dark-complexioned and muscular. Born on March 28, 1811, in Prachatitz, Bohemia, he arrived in the United States in 1836 with only one dollar in his pocket. A month later, he was ordained at St. Patrick's Church on Mott Street in New York City. He became an American citizen in 1848.

In 1852, Pope Pius IX made Neumann, age 41, bishop of Philadelphia. This was the largest diocese in the United States; there were 170,000 Catholics in 35,000 square miles in Pennsylvania, southern New Jersey, and Delaware. Neumann considered himself a poor administrator, yet his administrative accomplishments were astounding. He established the first Catholic parochial school system in the country and oversaw the construction of schools, churches, and asylums.

The process leading to canonization is a long and complicated one. Thirty-six years after his death, in 1896, Bishop Neumann was declared venerable. In 1963, he became the first male American citizen to be beatified, and on June 19, 1977, he was canonized as Saint John Neumann by Pope Paul VI.

OTHER RELIGIOUS FIRSTS

The first Moravian to come to America was George Boenisch, an evangelist who accompanied a group of Schwenkfelders to Pennsylvania. He arrived on September 22, 1734. The Schwenkfelders, followers of the teachings of 16th-century reformer Kaspar Schwenkfeld, had a large community in Montgomery County.

The first Moravian Easter service was held in Bethlehem, Northampton County, in 1742, according to historical documents. However, there is a good possibility that an earlier service was held either in Savannah, Georgia, or in Nazareth, Northampton County. A group of Moravians had lived temporarily in Nazareth before moving permanently to Bethlehem in 1741. They founded that city on Christmas Day of that year.

The first Evangelical Church conference occurred on November 15, 1807, at the home of Samuel Becker of Kleinfeltersville, Lebanon County. Attending were five itinerant ministers, three local preachers, and 20 class leaders and exhorters (givers of spiritual advice and comfort). Jacob Albright, who had founded the group in 1800, was elected bishop. The first Evangelical Church building in the United States was erected in 1816 in New Berlin, Union County.

St. George's Church in Shenandoah, established in 1872, was the first Lithuanian Catholic parish in the United States.

The oldest Slovak Roman Catholic parish in the Western Hemisphere is St. Joseph's in Hazleton, Luzerne County, founded in 1885 by the Reverend Ignatius Jaskovic.

St. George's Church in Shenandoah, Schuylkill County, was the first Lithuanian Catholic parish in the United States, established in 1872. Also in Shenandoah is the oldest Ukrainian parish in the nation, St. Michael's, established in 1884.

St. Michael's Church in Shenandoah is the oldest Ukrainian parish in the United States, established in 1884. The church shown here burned down in the 1980s and has since been rebuilt.

On August 6, 1936, aboard the German zeppelin *Hindenburg*, Father James Renshaw Cox, of St. Patrick's Church in Pittsburgh, conducted the first Catholic mass in an airship over the ocean.

FALLINGWATER: MANY ARCHITECTURAL FIRSTS

Frank Lloyd Wright ranks today as one of the world's greatest architects. The first building he designed in Pennsylvania was Fallingwater, the private home of Pittsburgh department store magnate Edgar J. Kaufmann and his wife. The Kaufmanns owned a tract of land called Bear Run in the Laurel Highlands of southern Fayette County. In 1934, they commissioned Wright to design a summer home for them. The following year, Wright vis-

Fallingwater, architect Frank Lloyd Wright's first creation in Pennsylvania. *Courtesy of the Western Pennsylvania Conservancy*

ited the property, drew sketches, and came up with one of the wildest innovations in the history of American architecture. He designed the house on top of, and around, a waterfall.

The backbone of the house is a four-story chimney built of layers of hard, gray sandstone anchoring cantilevered terraces made of reinforced concrete—the architect's first use of this material in a residence. The cantilever, a favorite trademark of Wright's, allows the structures to hang in the air without visible support. He compared it to outstretched arms or tree limbs growing from trunks.

Fallingwater contains several architectural firsts, including the first use of Dunlap foam rubber in the couch cushions and the first application of fluorescent lighting in a private residence.

Fallingwater was completed in 1939, and the Kaufmanns occupied it until 1963. It was then turned over to the Western Pennsylvania Conservancy as a memorial to Liliane and Edgar J. Kaufmann. Their son, Edgar J. Kaufmann, Jr., donated the property.

☞ *To Visit: Fallingwater*

The only way to see Fallingwater is by a guided tour. To arrange for a tour, call 724-329-8501.

Fallingwater
Mill Run, PA 15464

THE CONVERTIBLE-TOP BUILDING

The first large building in the country that had a retractable roof was the Civic Arena and Exhibit Hall in downtown Pittsburgh, dedicated on September 17, 1961. The domed roof, which has no interior support, is divided radially into eight leaves, two of which are stationary. The other six are anchored to a pin at the top as they roll along curved rails laid on a circular, reinforced concrete girder that rings the base of the roof. The dome can open or close electrically in two and a half minutes. Almost completely circular, the structure is 415 feet in diameter, 136 feet high at the center, and can hold 13,000 spectators at a basketball game and 15,000 at a rally. It sits on a five-acre site and cost $22 million to construct. The roof contains about 2,950 tons of structural steel. The first event held at the Pittsburgh Civic Arena was the Ice Capades, from September 18 to 30, 1961.

A Sporting Chance

Baseball as we know it today was invented in New York City in 1845, and the first formal club was the Knickerbockers. However, as early as 1832, Pennsylvanians were playing their own version of baseball on sandlots around Market Street in Philadelphia. There were never enough players to make up a full team because the local folks scorned and teased any young man who played on the sand, especially such a "silly, children's game."

Nevertheless, players from Philadelphia and Camden, New Jersey, organized the Olympic Town Ball Club of Philadelphia in 1833. They made their own balls and bats. By 1866, there were 48 baseball teams in Pennsylvania in such places as Renovo, York, Lancaster, Harrisburg, Allentown, and New Castle. During the Civil War, baseball gained in popularity. The 95th Pennsylvania Regiment team played against units from other northern states.

Pay Ball

Playing a sport for money was considered repulsive by American fans in the mid-1800s. Until baseball, that is. A few ball clubs decided to cash in on this popularity by charging admission to their games; afterwards, the players divided the receipts among themselves. Other clubs knew a good thing when they saw it and started taking money, too, although they used "creative bookkeeping" to hide payments to their players, including them in such entries as "miscellaneous expenses."

First Professional Baseball Player

One of the greatest second basemen in the early 1860s was Alfred J. Reach from London, England, who played for the Brooklyn Eckfords. In 1863, the Philadelphia Athletics (now the Oakland A's) offered Reach $25 a week as "expenses," making him the first professional player in baseball. The fans detested the idea of Reach getting a paycheck, but they soon changed their minds when the Athletics racked up winning seasons with scores like 101 to 8 and 162 to 14.

Reach saved his money, and after leaving the Athletics in 1876, he founded a sporting goods manufacturing company that bore his name. He went on to serve as president of the Philadelphia Phillies from 1883 to 1902. Reach died a multi-millionaire at the age of 87 in Atlantic City, New Jersey, in 1928.

First Cork Baseball

Throughout the 19th century, baseball was played with various types of hard, rubber balls with a canvas cover. But in 1909, Ben Shibe, a principal investor in Al Reach's sporting goods company, invented a ball with a cork center tightly wrapped with a fine grade of wool, then encased by a stitched canvas cover. This made for a livelier ball. In tribute to Shibe's innovation (or maybe it was his money), the old major league stadium in Philadelphia, Shibe Park, was named after him.

First Perfect Game

George Washington Bradley was an unheralded baseball hero. Born in Reading, Berks County, on July 13, 1850, he enlisted in the U.S. Army during the Civil War as a drummer. When the officers found out that he was only 12 years old, they promptly discharged him. He wound up in Philadelphia, where he learned the carriage-painting trade, got married, started a family, and played amateur baseball. Ben Shibe saw him play and recommended him to the Easton, Pennsylvania, professional team in 1875.

The following season, the St. Louis National League team hired Bradley. There, on July 15, 1876, he stepped on the mound to pitch against Boston. Not one Bean-towner reached first base, as Bradley pitched the first perfect game in baseball history. The following week, he hurled three shut-outs, three days in a row, against Hartford. The great Christy Mathewson of Factoryville, Wyoming County, pitched two shut-outs in two days for the New York Giants, but nobody ever matched Bradley's three-day feat.

After quitting baseball in 1890, Bradley joined the Philadelphia police force. And in 1930, at the age of 80, he reluctantly turned in his badge and retired. He died a year later.

FIRST NATIONAL BASEBALL CHAMPIONSHIP

Many clubs were paying a salary to all their players by 1871, so in that year they banded together and formed the National Association of Professional Baseball. The first national championship was won by the Philadelphia Athletics. Unfortunately, the organization had no clout; teams often did not show up for games and players switched teams whenever they wished. The silk-hatted umpires, usually unpaid, often lost control of the games, and some owners, such as "Boss" Tweed of the New York Mutuals, fixed games.

Enough was enough. In 1876, the owners disbanded the league and organized the National League of Professional Baseball Clubs, which set strict guidelines for both teams and players. The organization flourishes today as the National League. For the rest of the 19th century, the National League dominated professional baseball, but in 1900, the fledgling Western League reorganized itself into the American League and began to attract players and spectators away from the National League teams.

WORLD SERIES

At the turn of the century, the Pittsburgh Pirates were the top professional baseball team in the country, having won three National League pennants in a row. In 1903, the champions of the new American League were the Boston Pilgrims (later called the Boston Red Sox). Barney Dreyfuss of the Pirates and Henry Killilea of the Pilgrims agreed to a nine-game post-season series to determine the "world champion." The World Series was born!

The first ball of the first World Series was pitched on October 1, 1903, in Boston. Pittsburgh won three of the first four games played. But Boston turned it around by winning the next four games—and the series, five games to three. Boston's success was largely due to its great pitchers, Bill Dinneen and Cy Young. To this day, the pitcher judged to be the year's best is honored with the Cy Young Award.

FIRST BASEBALL HALL OF FAMERS

In 1936, the Baseball Writers of America chose the first five members of the Baseball Hall of Fame: Ty Cobb, Walter Johnson, Christy Mathewson, Babe Ruth, and Honus Wagner. Two of these all-time greats were Pennsylvanians: Christy Mathewson of Factoryville, Wyoming County, and Honus Wagner of Pittsburgh.

BASEBALL'S FIRST SUPERSTAR

During the late 1800s, the most reliable, fastest fire company in New York City was Company Number Six, which the public referred to as the Big Six. The New York Giants had a pitcher (1902 to 1915) who was so controlled and so consistently good that Sam Crane, reporter for the *New York*

Journal, called him "Big Six." He was Christy Mathewson. Crane wasn't the only one who admired him—practically every baseball fan did; he was the first baseball player to receive nationwide fame. He won 37 games in one season, more than any other pitcher in the National League. He held the record for the most put-outs and assists by a pitcher. He won 30 games three seasons in a row and was a 20-game winner 12 times straight. Mathewson's lifetime record: 373 games won, 138 lost.

College Superstar

Mathewson was born on August 12, 1880, in Factoryville, Wyoming County. At the age of 17, he enrolled in Bucknell University in Lewisburg, Union County. He was a good baseball player, but an even better football player. He drop-kicked field goals of such great length and accuracy that fans dubbed him "Old Gumboots." At Bucknell, "Matty" was president of his class, a member of the glee club, and in two literary societies. He was also a great checkers player.

After graduating, Matty was recruited by John J. McGraw for the New York Giants. His most shining hour was the 1905 World Series, where he faced the Philadelphia Athletics three times in six days and, like a machine, shut them out every time. He pitched 27 innings and allowed only 14 hits, walked 1, and struck out 18.

In 1916, Mathewson left the Giants to manage the Cincinnati Reds, but he quit the team two years later to join the army. The country was embroiled in World War I, and Matty wanted to do his part. He was commissioned an officer in the Chemical Corps. After the Armistice was signed, Matty entered a deserted trench in France and got a whiff of poison gas. Later, some experts claimed that this was the cause of Mathewson's tuberculosis. "Big Six" died seven years later, on October 7, 1925, at age 45. He's buried in Lewisburg, Union County, near his alma mater.

LITTLE LEAGUE BASEBALL

One day in the spring of 1938, Carl E. Stoltz of Williamsport, Lycoming County, decided to organize a baseball team for the boys in his neighborhood. He took a group to Memorial Park and laid out a scaled-down baseball diamond. Then Stoltz turned his attention to money—he approached no less than 56 local businesses to sponsor his team. The money didn't come easily, but finally, Floyd Mutchler of the Lycoming Dairy contributed $30. Lundy Lumber's and the Jumbo Pretzel Company's contributions followed, and on June 6, 1939, the first official Little League baseball game was played between teams sponsored by Lycoming Dairy and Lundy Lumber.

On March 7, 1940, Stoltz and three managers—Bert Bebble, George Bebble, and John Lindemuth—wrote the first constitution of Little League baseball. By 1946, there were 28 teams in Pennsylvania. In 1947, Stoltz organized the first Little League World Series between teams from Pennsylvania and New Jersey. The following year, the U.S. Rubber Company kicked in $5,000 for a larger tournament. Nationwide publicity

Here is some of the action that took place in one of the first Little League World Series tournaments held at the founding field in Williamsport. *Courtesy of the Peter J. McGovern Little League Baseball Museum, South Williamsport, PA*

in newsreels and magazines sparked a rapid expansion of teams. By 1953, there were 11,496 teams in 46 states.

Girls were finally admitted into the Little League in 1974. Today there are thousands of Little League teams throughout the world. And every year the Little League World Series is held at Carl E. Stoltz Field in South Williamsport.

THE KICKOFF OF PRO FOOTBALL

By the late 1880s, young men were joining athletic clubs, not just to play sports or keep in shape, but to rub elbows with the elite of high society, who found such clubs fashionable. One's climb up the social ladder, however, was linked to the club's success on the playing field.

In 1889, the Allegheny Athletic Association (AAA) was organized in North Pittsburgh. It excelled in one sport—football—because it had a couple of good players from Yale University, namely John Moorehead and O. D. Thompson. Since hiring professionals was considered unsportsmanlike, the association had come up with a scheme to recruit these quality players. The AAA allowed the Yale men free use of its facilities and gave them complimentary meals in its elegant dining hall in exchange for their services on the gridiron. This was the first step toward professional football in this country.

First "Professional" Football Game

The AAA finished its first football season in 1890 with a 3-2-1 record against some strong teams in western Pennsylvania, but it hadn't played what was to become its big rival, the old, established Pittsburgh Athletic Club (PAC). The PAC had a star player, William Kirschner, who had been put on the payroll as the club's physical education instructor. (Pittsburgh's sportswriters noted that the number of Kirschner's phys. ed. classes was cut in half during the football season, while his salary was doubled!) In 1891, the PAC, with Kirschner, won all its games. The following year, the public clamored for a game between the AAA and the PAC, and both clubs agreed to a match.

And so, under clouds of smoke from nearby steel plants, the PAC and AAA faced off at the PAC's field on October 21, 1892. Tempers flared when the PAC accused the AAA of deliberately injuring its star player, Kirschner. The AAA countered that Kirschner was a professional and should not be playing at all. The PAC argued that the AAA was paying some of its players with special favors and free meals. Then E. V. Paul, president of the AAA, retaliated, "I am willing to bet that the PAC used a professional and it's not Kirschner. It's Stayer, your new center."

"Stayer" turned out to be A. C. Read, former captain of the Penn State football squad. No one could ever prove that he had really been paid to play during that big game, but the PAC's use of such "imported talent" opened the door to hiring professionals.

By the way, this first football game using some paid players ended in a 6-6 tie. Afterwards, both clubs split $1,200 in gate receipts. They agreed on a rematch the following month.

Pudge, the Snake, and Sport

Over the next three weeks, both clubs acted like warring nations, secretly acquiring special "weapons" to defeat their opponent.

At the time, William Walter "Pudge" Heffelfinger, an All-American guard, and Knowlton "the Snake" Ames were the best football players anywhere, and they were playing for a club in Chicago. George Barbour, manager of the PAC, boarded a train for Chicago on November 7 with a bundle of money to offer Heffelfinger and Ames to join his club. Unbeknownst to Barbour, "Pudge" and "the Snake" had already gotten a telegram from Bill Kountz, manager of the AAA. While Barbour was chugging toward the Windy City, the two All-Americans were already in Pittsburgh, practicing with the AAA. They were soon joined by former Chicago teammates Ed Malley and Ben "Sport" Donnelly.

Rematch day was November 12, 1892. The minute both teams took to the field, the PAC protested that the AAA was using outsiders. "So what!" retorted Kountz of the AAA. "You guys used a Penn Stater last time." The game was delayed while both sides argued. Once they kicked off, the AAA, using Pudge, the Snake, and Sport, proceeded to pummel the PAC, 4-0. Afterwards, Malley, Ames, and Donnelly were given $25 for expenses. The AAA paid Heffelfinger $500 plus $25 for expenses, making him the first bona fide professional football player in history.

First Pro Football Contract

On October 4, 1893, halfback Grant Dilbert signed the first professional football contract. He agreed to play exclusively for the PAC for $50 a game. (This deal, like Heffelfinger's, was kept secret until the contract was found many years later.) Meanwhile, across town, the AAA had three "unsigned" salaried players on its team: Ollie Rafferty, Peter Wright, and Jim Cleve. After losing its opening game in 1893, the Alleghenys hired the first full-time coach in professional football—Ben "Sport" Donnelly.

THE SPREAD OF PRO FOOTBALL

Two years after the athletic clubs of Pittsburgh started to pay football players under the table, the Greensburg Athletic Club (GAC), in neighboring Westmoreland County, decided to recruit professionals. It lured Lawson Fiscus away from the Allegheny club in the fall of 1894. Fiscus was an unpaid star player for the Alleghenys and earned a living teaching school in South Fork, Cambria County. Fiscus accepted Greensburg's offer of $20 a game, making the GAC the world's third pro football team. Fiscus' teammates included Frank Hargrave, Tom Donohoe, Charles Jamison, Bill Theurer, Joseph Wentlin, Richard Coulter, Charles Copeland, W. C. L. Rayne, Ed Mechling, Tom Jamison, John Cribbs, and coach Lloyd Huff.

Pro Football Comes Out of the Locker

Until 1895, professional football players kept mum about being paid. Then along came John Brallier, an 18-year-old quarterback from Indiana Normal School, now Indiana University of Pennsylvania. Brallier stood five feet six inches and weighed 125 pounds sopping wet, but Dave Berry, manager of the Latrobe YMCA football squad, offered the kid $20 per game to play for the "Y." Not only did Brallier accept, he bragged openly to one and all that he was being paid. In the autumn of 1895, the Latrobe "Y" played against its neighbor team in Jeannette, Westmoreland County. The players on both teams were paid $10 each. This game was promoted as the first "fully professional football game in history."

WHO WAS PAID FIRST?

John Brallier's openness about being paid to play got him recognized as the very first professional football player. In 1960 (ironically, the year Brallier died), Nelson Ross, who was doing some research on football, came across an 1892 account ledger prepared by O. D. Thompson for the Allegheny Athletic Association. Included was this entry: "Game performance bonus to W. Heffelfinger for playing—cash $500." Ross gave the information to Art Rooney, owner of the Pittsburgh Steelers, and Rooney had the data checked by scholars, who proved it valid. Thus, a 68-year-old expense account shattered the late John Brallier's bragging rights and confirmed "Pudge" Heffelfinger as the first pro footballer.

FIRST FOOTBALL LEAGUE

At the turn of the century, professional baseball was well established and the two leagues—the National and the American—were constantly stealing players from one another. Nowhere was this athletic thievery more prevalent than in Philadelphia, where the National League's Phillies and the American League's Athletics were preoccupied with pirating each other's players.

In 1902, Phillies owner John I. Rogers organized a football team. Not to be outdone, Ben Shibe, majority owner of the Athletics, asked his manager, Connie Mack, to team up with former University of Pennsylvania tackle Blondy Wallace and assemble a stronger gridiron team. But the best players were in the western part of the state, so Shibe and Rogers contacted Dave Berry, former manager of the Latrobe "Y." Berry was familiar with the best team in the area, the Homestead Library and Athletic Club, which had finished the previous season with 11 wins and no losses. Situated next to Pittsburgh on the south side of the Monongahela River, the town of Homestead was the site of the largest steel plant in the world during the early part of the 20th century. Thus, the town's gridiron club was called the Homestead Steelers. Plagued by financial losses, the Steelers were about to break up when Berry stepped in and took over. He renamed the club the Pittsburgh Steelers. Thus, Berry, Shibe, and Rogers formed the first league of professional football teams—the National Football League.

These three teams openly admitted they were pros, and they invited other teams to join their league. Other states followed suit and formed their own leagues. The National Football League, as we know it today, was organized in 1920 at the Hupmobile dealership in Canton, Ohio, by the owner of the Canton Bulldogs. Their first president was a former Pennsylvania resident and namesake of a town in Carbon County—Jim Thorpe.

FIRST NIGHT FOOTBALL GAME

On September 29, 1892, 20 electric lights, totaling 2,000 candlepower, were hooked up to a Thompson & Huston Dynamo Machine at the Mansfield Fair in Tioga County. A football game was then played between the Mansfield State Teachers College and the Wyoming Seminary of Kingston, Luzerne County. The game lasted 70 minutes, half of which was played under the lights. It ended in a scoreless tie.

Armor, William C. *Lives of the Governors of Pennsylvania.* Philadelphia: James K. Simon, 1873.

Astor, Gerald. *The Baseball Hall of Fame 50th Anniversary Book.* New York: Prentice Hall, 1988.

Beers, Paul. *Profiles of the Susquehanna Valley.* Harrisburg: Stackpole Books, 1973.

Elroy, Janice H. *Our Hidden Heritage: Pennsylvania Women in History.* Washington, D.C.: American Association of University Women, 1984.

Giddens, Paul H. *Early Days of Oil.* Princeton: Princeton University Press, 1948.

Honing, Donald. *Baseball: The Illustrated History of America's Game.* New York: Crown Publishing, 1990.

Picture History of Lycoming County, A. Vol. 2. N.p.: Commissioners of Lycoming County, 1969.

Ramsaye, Terry. *A Million and One Nights.* New York: Simon & Schuster, 1926.

Shank, William H. *Vanderbilt's Folly.* York, Pa.: American Canal & Transportation Center, 1973.

Smith, Frank Kingston. *Legacy of Wings: The Harold F. Pitcairn Story.* Lafayette Hill, Pa.: TD Associates, 1981.

Spencer, Herbert. *Erie: A History.* N.p.: published by the author, 1962.

Stevens, Sylvester, Ralph Cordier, and Florence Benjamin. *Exploring Pennsylvania.* New York: Harcourt Brace, 1963.

Swetnam, George. *Pennsylvania Transportation.* Gettysburg: Pennsylvania Historical Association, 1968.

Wallace, Paul A. *Indians in Pennsylvania.* Harrisburg: Pennsylvania Historical & Museum Commission, 1968.

Works Progress Administration Writers Program. *Pennsylvania: A Guide to the Keystone State.* New York: Oxford University Press, 1963.